D1084508

Motor Coordination Disorders in Children

Developmental Clinical Psychology and Psychiatry Series

Series Editor: Alan E. Kazdin, Yale University

Recent volumes in this series . . .

Motor Coordination Disorders in Children

David A. Sugden
Helen C. Wright

Volume 39
Developmental Clinical Psychology and Psychiatry

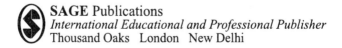

SAGE Publications
International Educational and Professional Publisher
Thousand Oaks   London   New Delhi

For information:

SAGE Publications, Inc.
2455 Teller Road
Thousand Oaks, California 91320
E-mail: order@sagepub.com

SAGE Publications Ltd.
6 Bonhill Street
London EC2A 4PU
United Kingdom

SAGE Publications India Pvt. Ltd.
M-32 Market
Greater Kailash I
New Delhi 110 048 India

RJ496
.M68
S84
1998

Printed in the United States of America

Library of Congress Cataloging-in-Publication Data

Sugden, David A.
    Motor coordination disorders in children / by David A. Sugden and
Helen C. Wright.
        p. cm. — (Developmental clinical psychology and psychiatry ; v. 39)
    Includes bibliographical references and index.
    ISBN 0-7619-0999-0 (cloth: acid-free paper)
    1. Clumsiness in children. 2. Motor ability in children.
    I. Wright, Helen C., 1956- II. Title. III. Series.
RJ496.M68 S84 1998
618.92′7—ddc21

                                          98-19704

This book is printed on acid-free paper.

98 99 00 01 02 03 04 7 6 5 4 3 2 1

Acquisition Editor:	Jim Nageotte
Editorial Assistant:	Heidi Van Middlesworth
Production Editor:	Wendy Westgate
Editorial Assistant:	Denise Santoyo
Typesetter:	Christina M. Hill
Cover Designer:	Candice Harman

CONTENTS

SERIES EDITOR'S INTRODUCTION

Interest in child development and adjustment is by no means new. Yet only recently has the study of children benefited from advances in both clinical and scientific research. Advances in the social and biological sciences; the emergence of disciplines and subdisciplines that focus exclusively on childhood and adolescence; and greater appreciation of the impact of such influences as the family, peers, and school have helped accelerate research on developmental psychopathology. Apart from interest in the study of child development and adjustment for its own sake, the need to address clinical problems of adulthood naturally draws one to investigate precursors in childhood and adolescence.

Within a relatively brief period, the study of psychopathology among children and adolescents has proliferated considerably. Several different professional journals, annual book series, and handbooks devoted entirely to the study of children and adolescents and their adjustment document the proliferation of work in the field. Nevertheless, there is a paucity of resource material that presents information in an authoritative, systematic, and disseminable fashion. There is a need within the field to convey the latest developments and to represent different disciplines, approaches, and conceptual views to the topics of childhood and adolescent adjustment and maladjustment.

The Sage series **Developmental Clinical Psychology and Psychiatry** is designed to serve uniquely several needs of the field. The series encompasses individual monographs prepared by experts in the fields of clinical child psychology, child psychiatry, child development, and related disciplines. The primary focus is on developmental psychopathology, which refers broadly here to the diagnosis, assessment, treatment, and prevention of problems that arise in the period from infancy through adolescence. A working assumption of the series is that understanding, identifying, and treating problems of youth must draw on multiple disciplines and diverse views within a given discipline.

The task for individual contributors is to present the latest theory and research on various topics, including specific types of dysfunction, diagnostic and treatment approaches, and special problem areas that affect adjustment. Core topics within clinical work are addressed by the series. Authors are asked to bridge potential theory, research, and clinical practice and to outline the current status and future directions. The goals of the Series and the tasks presented to individual contributors are demanding. We have been extremely fortunate in recruiting leaders in the fields who have been able to translate their recognized scholarship and expertise into highly readable works on contemporary topics.

In this book, David A. Sugden and Helen C. Wright examine *Motor Coordination Disorders in Children*. Among currently recognized childhood disorders in contemporary psychiatric diagnosis, perhaps none is as intriguing as motor coordination disorders in underscoring the dynamic interrelations of biological, psychological, and social development. Children with motor coordination disorders often show impairment in emotional, behavioral, and social domains that overlap significantly with characteristics of children with other disorders. Moreover, motor disorders are readily overlooked because of lack of familiarity with their diagnosis and assessment methods. This book examines the nature of the disorders, developmental progressions, associated features, and long-term prognoses. Drs. Sugden and Wright address etiology, methods of assessment, and interventions. The book reviews issues related to identification and description of the disorders, current research findings, and controversies and challenges for research and clinical work. Key questions remain about the onset and characteristics of the disorders and the mechanisms through which problems of motor coordination may relate to impairment in other domains of functioning. The authors have contributed significantly to research on motor coordination disorders and are in a unique position to provide an authoritative account of the topic.

ALAN E. KAZDIN, PHD

PREFACE

The literature on children with motor coordination disorders has been steadily accumulating since the early 1960s. This literature, originally focusing on characteristics of so-called clumsy children or the clumsy child syndrome, now encompasses children with a range of labels, the most recent being *developmental coordination disorder.* The original descriptive studies have been complemented by longitudinal, experimental, and case studies together in school and home. Studies on identification, assessment, characteristics, and nature of the disorder are most prevalent, but management and intervention investigations are now becoming more commonplace.

Our aim in this text is to capture the available literature on motor disorders in children and examine it critically alongside our knowledge of children's motor development. The children we are discussing are those with motor difficulties but who have no overt constitutional disorder. We recognize the hazy confusion surrounding etiology and biology and accept that, in some children we discuss, underlying constitutional origins may be present but not identified. However, our focus is on those children without such disorders and in turn have been labeled "clumsy," "awkward," "maladroit," "dyspraxic," and other terms.

We are hoping to address issues that are of interest to those individuals who come into contact with children showing motor disorders. Thus, the book is aimed at professionals, including teachers, physiotherapists, occupational therapists, psychologists, and pediatricians, and of course, parents of such children, a group often neglected or ill-informed in the ecology of any disorder. The text is not one that guides professionals through how-to-do-it situations. It is a text that elaborates, highlights, and discusses the many issues surrounding motor disorders in children. It tries to answer questions such as these: What does the condition look like? Is it a simple syndrome or are there subgroups showing heterogeneous characteristics? How do we assess? How does the condition progress? Is intervention successful? We have selected these and other issues to focus our efforts on rather than present exhaustive and comprehensive accounts of all that has been written.

In Chapter 1, we address general issues, such as terminology and definition, noting how different professionals have viewed the disorder. An overview of its development and progression illustrates the pervasive nature of the disorder and its associated effects. General motor development is covered in Chapter 2. In the first part, the course of motor development is described and illustrated by a selective examination of manual and locomotor skills. In the second part, the more difficult task of explaining the course of motor development is attempted. Traditional explanations involving maturation and information-processing systems are covered before settling on explanations based on dynamic systems theory. Accurate identification and assessment are essential to the eventual specific and targeted intervention with any disorder, and motor disability is no exception. In Chapter 3, we examine general assessment issues, attempting to categorize the various types and outline a number of assessment instruments currently available. Full descriptions of the nature of the disorder are presented in Chapter 4. The first part examines the traditional literature on intergroup differences, that is, differences between children with motor disorders and controls. The second part examines the intragroup characteristics and is a more recent development recognizing that these children do not form an homogeneous group. When we examine the progression and development of the disorder in Chapter 5, we divide it into two parts. The first examines the period from birth to 6 or 7 years of age and analyzes the relationship between early life variables and outcomes as children enter school. The second part looks at 6 or 7 to 16 or 17 years of age examining the course of the disorder and the variables that may have had an intervening effect on its progress. Chapter 6 examines approaches to intervention, and again, the chapter divides into two parts. The first is known as task-oriented and directly addresses those skills on which the child is failing or is thought to need. The second is known as process-oriented and examines those processes such as sensory input, kinesthesis, feedback, and vision, which are thought to underlie skilled motor performance. A final chapter highlights major issues addressed throughout the book.

Any text is not solely due to the efforts of its authors, and thanks are due to a number of others. David Sugden would particularly like to thank Sheila Henderson for the friendship, discussions, exchanges, and work they have engaged in over the last 20 years. His thanks also go to Jack Keogh, who introduced him to the area, for the friendship and work over a 27-year period, including two books, several hundred bottles of fine wine, and a few rounds of terrible but enjoyable golf. Last, to his wife, Lorrie, go his thanks and love for this and other works, for without her support and her "you get on with the book I will sort it" approach to life, none would have been possible. Helen Wright notes that at home, her loving and stalwart supporter, Daniel Soucie, was ever present, ready with words of advice and encouragement. No text such as this can be achieved without the help of those you cherish, and so with great pride, she dedicates her efforts to Daniel.

1

DEVELOPMENTAL
COORDINATION DISORDER

HISTORICAL ASPECTS

Children with motor coordination disorders have attracted attention from a wide range of professionals, the early investigations often involving the medical profession with pediatricians and neurologists taking an interest. An article titled "Clumsy Children" (1962) appeared in the *British Medical Journal* in December 1962, chronicling behavior seen in school children that could mistakenly be attributed to naughtiness or low intelligence but was more likely to be a consequence of poor motor skills. The paper highlighted ongoing independent works in Sweden, The Netherlands, and Great Britain that were suggesting a syndrome of behaviors that had no clear link to any known neurological disorder. The disorder, found not uncommonly in young primary school age children, resulted in a marked impairment in the performance of functional skills required to succeed at school. Impaired motor performance by this age group had of course been noticed before the paper in the *British Medical Journal,* but this paper possibly marked the beginning of published works that adopted a scientific approach to the study of what we recognize today as *developmental coordination disorder* (DCD). This paper called for concerted study to be undertaken to maximize the opportunities to help children with DCD.

In 1962, Walton, Ellis, and Court (1962) attempted, through descriptive processes, to come to terms with a syndrome of motor difficulties they were noticing in young children referred to them through medical channels. They noted that the motor difficulties these children demonstrated were "a great disability and interfered seriously with their education" (p. 603).

The purpose of their paper was to expose this syndrome, which they felt was not uncommon yet often overlooked. They noted that they were unable to find any satisfactory account of similar cases in the medical literature, and this paper was an attempt to fill the gap in the literature. Five children were reported on and found to suffer from severe clumsiness as the main feature of their disorder and to such a degree that many motor activities essential to everyday life were distinctly impaired. Walton et al. (1962) could find no trace of defects in the pyramidal, extrapyramidal, or cerebellar pathways that control volitional motor activity. They hypothesized that the difficulties seen in these children occurred because of a defect in cerebral organization and not from an acquired pathological lesion of any single area of the brain. They also noted that distinguishing the cause of this apparent syndrome was not simple, but they refuted the notion that the difficulties evidenced by the children were a consequence of abnormal maturation that could be corrected with the passing of time. The persistence of the children's difficulties, seen in their apraxic and agnosic disorders, was recorded as stubborn. In summary, Walton et al. (1962) stated that apraxic and agnosic disorders, although known in children with cerebral palsy, can also occur as isolated difficulties without other signs of neurological disturbance.

As a clearer picture of the motor difficulties faced by children with DCD has emerged, interest and research in the subject have spread from medical personnel to psychologists, educationalists, and therapists. These professionals are united not only in their quest for an understanding of the condition but equally important, in how to deal with and help children overcome their difficulties.

TERMINOLOGY

Many terms and titles have been used to describe DCD. Often, the descriptors used have revealed the emphases of the researchers' interests. Medical personnel use medical terms, whereas educationalists more often use more basic terms, such as *clumsy* or *awkward,* although the medical profession also began by using the term *clumsy.* Each term sheds light on the difficulties experienced by children with movement difficulties.

The following terms have been used: *clumsy children* (Dare & Gordon, 1970; Geuze & Kalverboer, 1994; Henderson, 1987; Keogh, Sugden, Reynard, & Calkins, 1979; Lord & Hulme, 1987b; Losse et al., 1991; and many others); *clumsy child syndrome,* (Gubbay, 1975b); *coordination problems or difficulties* (O'Beirne, Larkin, & Cable, 1994; Sugden & Henderson, 1994); *motor coordination problems or difficulties* (Maeland, 1992; Roussounis, Gaussen, & Stratton, 1987); *movement skills problems* (Sugden & Sugden,

1991); *movement problems or difficulties* (Henderson, May, & Umney, 1989; Sugden & Keogh, 1990; Wright, Sugden, Ng, & Tan, 1994); *preceptuo-motor dysfunction* (Laszlo, Bairstow, Bartrip, & Rolfe, 1988); *dyspraxia* (Henderson & Sugden, 1991; Iloeje, 1987; McGovern, 1991; Walton et al., 1962); *developmental coordination disorder* (American Psychiatric Association [APA], 1987, 1992; Henderson, 1992; Hoare, 1994; Missiuna, 1994; Mon-Williams, Wann, & Pascual, 1994; Sugden & Wright, 1995, 1996; World Health Organization [WHO] 1992a, 1992b, 1993; Wright, 1997; plus many others).

This is by no means an exhaustive list of descriptors and researchers in the field of DCD, but it is a reflection of the number of terms that are used interchangeably in articles published around the world.

CORE FEATURES

The extent to which the descriptors differ is a testament to the heterogeneity of the difficulties experienced by children with DCD. Not only are the differences in children with DCD revealed in their range, but the pervasiveness of the problem differs from child to child. For certain children, their difficulties may only be evident in fine motor tasks or only in gross motor tasks. It could be that the environment limits or affords the child's movement control. When the environment is stable and the child is stationary, few problems emerge. However, if or when the timing of tasks shifts to include the presence of others, such as in catching a ball, tasks have to be adapted, and the child's difficulties are more clearly seen. For other children, their lack of motor control is evident in every sphere, although in some cases less severely than in others (Hoare, 1994; Wright & Sugden, 1996a). The sources of the difficulties are numerous and can be unidimensional or multidimensional. The child's difficulties could arise from poor planning, a lack of understanding, or a cognitive difficulty with the task and how it fits in with other movements.

The overall picture of a child who has DCD shows that to a degree, the basic fundamental skills of reaching, grasping, sitting, standing, walking, and running have emerged. However, the necessary development into competent functional skills, which enable children to manipulate and control their environments, has not occurred (Henderson, 1992). This lack of development means that, by comparison, children with DCD fall behind their peers in some or all of these functional skills, resulting in a detrimental effect on their progress at school.

CLASSIFICATION

The term developmental coordination disorder appears in both the APA's *Diagnostic and Statistical Manual of Mental Disorders* (DSM) and the WHO (1992a, 1992b, 1993) *International Classification of Diseases and Related Health Problems* (ICD-10). DCD was first classified as such in DSM-III-R (APA, 1987), the third edition, revised, of the DSM. The classifications in these manuals represent a very positive step forward, not only in terms of recognition for the disorder but also, because of the credibility these manuals offer. The fact that DCD now has a specific entry and is regarded as a separable developmental disorder of motor skills means that it requires diagnostic, etiological, and remedial attention in its own right (Henderson, 1994). The concept of people worldwide using the same term, DCD, can only be of help in understanding the nature of the disorder and in dealing with its management across cultures and national divides. As we have described, DCD has been given many titles over the years, some pejorative, others not, but with so many descriptors accredited to the disorder, some confusion is inevitable. Establishing common ground through the acceptance of a name for a disorder has positive, practical implications. Children with DCD can be distinguished from children with other difficulties, such as dyslexia, cerebral palsy, or hyperactivity. However, it is recognized that overlap of symptoms is a regular feature of many childhood disorders, and this is no exception.

The latest entry in DSM-IV (APA, 1994) and the ICD-10 (WHO, 1992a, 1992b, 1993) entries are presented completely to facilitate a clearer understanding of the classifications as they currently stand. The entry for APA (1994) is titled "Developmental Coordination Disorder," whereas in the WHO (1992a, 1992b, 1993) publication, DCD is among a number of terms used within their title of "Specific developmental disorder of motor function."

Similarities and Differences in DSM-IV and ICD-10

Examining the given classifications, certain aspects of DCD are highlighted in both manuals, but at the same time, there are aspects that are absent in one or other citations and also, explanations that are different. The first example of a difference is in the title attributed to the disorder. The DSM-IV (APA, 1994) names the disorder quite clearly "developmental coordination disorder," offering no other name to be equated with this. ICD-10 (WHO, 1992a, 1992b, 1993) titles its classification "specific developmental disorder of motor function," with DCD being one of three related terms used to describe the disorder. The other options are "clumsy child syndrome" and

1.1 DSM-IV Description of DCD

Motor Skills Disorder

315.4 Developmental Coordination Disorder

Diagnostic Features

The Essential Feature of Developmental Coordination

Disorder is a marked impairment in the development of motor coordination (Criterion A). The diagnosis is made only if this impairment significantly interferes with academic achievement or activities of daily living (Criterion B). The diagnosis is made if the coordination difficulties are not due to a general medical condition (e.g., cerebral palsy, hemiplegia, or muscular dystrophy) and the criteria are not met for Pervasive Developmental Disorder (Criterion C). If Mental Retardation is present, the motor difficulties are in excess of those usually associated with it (Criterion D). The manifestations of this disorder vary with age and development. For example, younger children may display clumsiness and delays in achieving developmental motor milestones (e.g., walking, crawling, sitting, tying shoelaces, buttoning shirts, zipping pants). Older children may display difficulties with the motor aspects of assembling puzzles, building models, playing ball, and printing or handwriting.

Associated Features and Disorders

Problems commonly associated with Developmental Coordination Disorder include delays in other nonmotor milestones. Associated disorders may include Phonological Disorder, Expressive Language Disorder, and Mixed Receptive-Expressive Language Disorder.

Prevalence

Prevalence of Developmental Coordination Disorder has been estimated to be as high as 6% for children in the age range of 5-11 years.

Course

Recognition of Developmental Coordination Disorder usually occurs when the child first attempts such tasks as running, holding a knife and fork, buttoning clothes, or playing ball games. The course is variable. In some cases, lack of coordination continues through adolescence and adulthood.

Differential Diagnosis

Developmental Coordination Disorder must be distinguished from motor impairments that are due to a general medical condition. Problems in coordination may be associated with **specific neurological disorders** (e.g., cerebral palsy, progressive lesions of the cerebellum), but in these cases there is a definite neural damage and abnormal findings on neurological examination. If **Mental Retardation** is present, Developmental Coordination Disorder can be diagnosed only if the motor difficulties are in excess of those usually associated with the Mental Retardation. A diagnosis of Developmental Coordination Disorder is not given if the criteria are met for a **Pervasive Developmental Disorder**. Individuals with **Attention-Deficit/Hyperactivity Disorder** may fall, bump into things, or knock things over, but this is usually due to distractibility and impulsiveness, rather than to motor impairment. If criteria for both disorders are met, both diagnoses can be given.

Diagnostic criteria for 315.4 Developmental Coordination Disorder

A. Performance in daily activities that require motor coordination is substantially below that expected given the person's chronological age and measured intelligence. This may be manifested by marked delays in achieving motor milestones (e.g., walking, crawling, sitting), dropping things, "clumsiness," poor performance in sports, or poor handwriting.

B. The disturbance in Criterion A significantly interferes with academic achievement or activities of daily living.

C. The disturbance is not due to a general medical condition (e.g., cerebral palsy, hemiplegia, or muscular dystrophy) and does not meet the criteria for a Pervasive Developmental Disorder.

D. If Mental Retardation is present, the motor difficulties are in excess of those usually associated with it.

SOURCE: APA (1994, pp. 53-55). Reprinted with permission from the *Diagnostic and Statistical Manual of Mental Disorders, Fourth Edition.* Copyright 1994 American Psychiatric Association.

1.2   ICD-10 (1992a) Description of DCD

| F82 | **Specific developmental disorder of motor function** |

A disorder in which the main feature is a serious impairment in the development of motor coordination that is not solely explicable in terms of general intellectual retardation or of any specific congenital or acquired neurological disorder. Nevertheless, in most cases a careful clinical examination shows marked neuro-developmental immaturities such as choreiform movements of unsupported limbs or mirror movements and other associated motor features, as well as signs of impaired fine and gross motor coordination.

Clumsy child syndrome
Developmental:
• coordination disorder
• dyspraxia
Excludes: abnormalities of gait and mobility (R26.-)
        lack of coordination (R27.-)
        • secondary to mental retardation (F70-F79)

SOURCE: WHO (1992a), reprinted with permission.

1.3 ICD-10 (1992b) Description of DCD

F82

Specific developmental disorder of motor function

The main feature of this disorder is a serious impairment in the development of motor coordination that is not solely explicable in terms of general intellectual retardation or of any specific congenital or acquired neurological disorder (other than the one that may be implicit in the coordination abnormality). It is usual for the motor clumsiness to be associated with some degree of impaired performance on visuo-spatial cognitive tasks.

Diagnostic guidelines
The child's motor coordination, on fine or gross motor tasks, should be significantly below the level expected on the basis of his or her age and general intelligence. This is best assessed on the basis of an individually administered, standardized test of fine and gross motor coordination. The difficulties in co-ordination should have been present since early in development (i.e., they should not constitute an acquired deficit), and they should not be a direct result of any defects of vision or hearing or of any diagnosable neurological disorder.

The extent to which the disorder mainly involves fine or gross motor coordination varies, and the particular pattern of motor disabilities varies with age. Developmental motor milestones may be delayed and there may be some associated speech difficulties (especially involving articulation). The young child may be awkward in general gait, being slow to learn to run, hop, and go up and down stairs. There is likely to be difficulty learning to tie shoe laces, to fasten and unfasten buttons, and to throw and catch balls. The child may be generally clumsy in fine and/or gross movements—tending to drop things, to stumble, to bump into obstacles, and to have poor handwriting. Drawing skills are usually poor, and children with this disorder are often poor at jigsaw puzzles, using constructional toys, building models, ball games, and drawing and understanding maps.

In most cases a careful clinical examination shows marked neurodevelopmental immaturities such as choreiform movements of unsupported limbs, or mirror movements and other associated motor features, as well as signs of poor fine or gross motor coordination (generally described as "soft" neurological signs because of their normal occurrence in younger children and their lack of localizing value). Tendon reflexes may be increased or decreased bilaterally but will not be asymmetrical.

Scholastic difficulties occur in some children and may occasionally be severe; in some cases, there are associated socio-emotional behavioral problems, but little is known of their frequency or characteristics.

There is no diagnosable neurological disorder (such as cerebral palsy or muscular dystrophy). In some cases, however, there is a history of perinatal complications, such as low birth weight or markedly premature birth. The clumsy child syndrome has been diagnosed as "minimal brain dysfunction," but this term is not recommended as it has so many different and contradictory meanings.

Includes: clumsy child syndrome
developmental coordination disorder
developmental dyspraxia
Excludes: abnormalities of gait and mobility (R26.-)
lack of coordination (R27.-) secondary to either mental retardation
(F70-F79) or some specific diagnosable neurological disorder (G00-G99)

SOURCE: WHO (1992b), reprinted with permission.

1.4 ICD-10 (1993) Description of DCD

| F82 | **Specific developmental disorder of motor function** |

A.   The score on a standardized test of fine or gross motor coordination is at least 2 standard deviations below the level expected for the child's chronological age.
B.   The disturbance described in criterion A significantly interferes with academic achievement or with activities of daily living.
C.   There is no diagnosable neurological disorder.
D.   *Most commonly used exclusion clause.* IQ is below 70 on an individually administered standardized test.

SOURCE: WHO (1993), reprinted with permission.

"developmental dyspraxia." No mention is made of how these terms may relate to each other, if they do at all, or whether they may be used interchangeably. However, as far as the diagnostic features and differential diagnoses are concerned, the two classifications demonstrate agreement. Both state that there is a marked (DSM-IV) or serious (ICD-10) impairment in the development of motor coordination and that this interferes significantly with academic life or in DSM-IV, daily living skills or both. Both note that the child's movements are awkward and clumsy and that the disorder is not due to a diagnosable medical condition such as cerebral palsy. For the condition to be recognized in a person who is mentally retarded, the lack of coordination must be in excess of what is expected. ICD-10 goes as far as to say that all persons with an IQ of less than 70 should be excluded from this diagnosis.

With regards to the existence of a medical condition, both classifications clearly conclude what DCD is not by eliminating certain conditions. However, ICD-10 (WHO, 1992b) ventures farther into the medical sphere to state

> In most cases a careful clinical examination shows marked neurodevelopmental immaturities such as choreiform movements of unsupported limbs, or mirror movements and other associated motor features, as well as signs of poor fine or gross motor coordination (generally described as "soft" neurological signs because of their occurrence in younger children and their lack of localizing value). Tendon reflexes may be increased or decreased bilaterally but will not be asymmetrical. (p. 250)

In addition, ICD-10 (WHO, 1992b) recognizes that perinatal complications such as low birth weight or premature births may be linked to DCD and suggests a link between the clumsy child syndrome and "minimal brain dysfunction," although the term is not recommended due to its many different and contradictory meanings.

Both citations mention the existence of features associated with DCD such as delays in the achievement of nonmotor milestones, for example, language development. However, only ICD-10 (WHO, 1992b) states that these features may include "associated socio-emotional behavioral problems" (p. 250). Although DSM-IV (APA, 1994) could be said to be less detailed and specific in its description of DCD, it does remark on the course of the disorder and the prevalence rate, neither of which are discussed by ICD-10 (WHO, 1992a, 1992b, 1993). The method of assessment and the severity of DCD are not dealt with by DSM-IV (APA, 1994), but the ICD-10 (WHO, 1993) statement advises the use of a standardized test of fine and gross motor coordination to assess DCD, where the child scores at least two standard deviations below the expected level for the child's age. Together, these two classifications, despite their differences, do inform the reader as to the nature of DCD, although more is known about the disorder than is included. Comments on the inclusions and exclusions from DSM-IV (APA, 1994) and ICD-10 (1992a, 1992b, 1993) follow in the next section.

Analysis of the Classifications

Although the APA (1994) and WHO (1992a, 1992b, 1993) classifications do offer official acceptance of DCD as a disorder with some clear statements, there are ambiguous points, too. For example, both classifications are very clear that DCD is not the result of "a general medical condition" (APA, 1994,

p. 53) or a "diagnosable neurological disorder" (WHO, 1992b, p. 251), yet when it comes to the criteria for diagnosis, less clear terms are used, such as, "Performance in daily activities that require motor coordination is substantially below that expected given the person's chronological age and measured intelligence" (APA, 1994, p. 54) and, "The child's motor coordination, on fine or gross motor tasks, should be significantly below the level expected on the basis of his or her age and intelligence" (WHO, 1992b, p. 250).

These descriptions may lead a reader to presume that DCD is solely related to poor overt motor skill functions and that affected children with DCD demonstrate these difficulties across the board or in fine or gross motor skills. This precludes the possibility that the difficulties could arise from poor planning, poor spatial or temporal awareness, or poor kinesthetic awareness. ICD-10 (WHO, 1992b) does include the statement that it is usual for the clumsiness to be linked with impaired visuospatial cognitive performance. However, the terms used by ICD-10 could be criticized for their lack of clarity.

The emphasis on the product of motor performance does detract from substantial clinical experience and reporting on the planning aspect of motor behavior. Although the term dyspraxia is often used as a synonym for DCD or clumsiness, it is also widely used to represent a child with planning difficulties, and indeed, apraxia is a well-documented adult motor disorder. Thus, a child may have adequate motor control, but when asked to perform a task such as folding a letter, putting it in an envelope, and then placing it is a letter box, the child may show numerous difficulties. This could involve a difficulty in orienting the letter so that it can be folded with one or two folds, or it could involve an error in the sequence of events, such sticking down the envelope before the letter is put in. This type of child is usually placed under the broad heading of DCD or dyspraxia, making it essential that accurate diagnosis of the specific problem is carried out.

An exact description of the disorder is difficult, but it is becoming clearer that there is an enormous range not only in the severity of DCD but also in the difficulties that the children experience (Barnett, 1992; Dewey & Kaplan, 1994; Hoare, 1994; Wright & Sugden, 1996a).

Longitudinal studies have shown that without intervention, the difficulties seen in early years can still be found in teenage years (Cantell, Ahonen, & Smyth, 1994; Geuze & Börger, 1993; Losse et al., 1991; Lyytinen & Ahonen, 1989). DSM-IV (APA, 1994) briefly states that "The course [of DCD] is variable. In some cases, lack of coordination continues through adolescence and adulthood" (p. 54), whereas ICD-10 (WHO, 1992a, 1992b, 1993) makes no reference at all to the developmental course of DCD. Both classifications emphasize that academic achievement or the activities of daily living or both are disturbed and interfered with, but the details of these detrimental effects are not forthcoming. Yet there is evidence that children with DCD are negatively affected in the areas of goal setting, self-concept, locus of control (Henderson et al., 1989), self-esteem (Shaw, Levine, & Belfer, 1982), and experience social and affective problems (Schoemaker & Kalverboer, 1994). These studies have shown that having DCD is not an isolated problem solely including motor skills but that the disorder also has an effect on social and affective functioning. Schoemaker, Hijklema, and Kalverboer (1994) found that if children with DCD were treated with a physiotherapy program, the long-term beneficial effects were evident in not only the motor domain but also the social and affective domains. Wright and Sugden (1997) also report that teachers found a concomitant improvement in associated behaviors, with improved motor function, through a school-based intervention program.

There are further contentious points when considering the APA (1994) and WHO (1992a, 1992b, 1993) classifications. One area is the necessity for a clear statement about normative referencing rather than the present statements that offer little idea of relaed competencies. ICD-10 (WHO, 1993) notes that DCD is diagnosed if a child scores at least 2 standard deviations below the level expected for his or her chronological age on a standardized test of fine and gross motor coordination. DSM-IV (APA, 1994) simply states that "The diagnosis is made only if this impairment significantly interferes with academic or activities of daily living" (p. 53). Exactly what standardized tests should be used is not information supplied by ICD-10 (WHO, 1993) nor is the term "significantly interferes" explained in DSM-IV (APA, 1994).

The prevalence of DCD is estimated in DSM-IV (APA, 1994), where the figure quoted for children aged 5 to 11 years is "as high as 6%" (p. 54). ICD-10 (WHO, 1992a, 1992b, 1993) makes no mention of a prevalence rate for the disorder. Figures from around the world show that the prevalence rate varies from 2.7% to 15.6% (2.7%—The Netherlands, van Dellen, Vaessen, & Schoemaker, 1990; 5.9%—Nigeria, Iloeje, 1987; 6.7%—Australia, Gubbay, 1975a; 10%—UK, Henderson, Rose, & Henderson, 1992; up to 15.6%—Singapore, Wright et al., 1994). These figures are subject to definitional difficulties, use of varying criteria, as well as use of different instruments to identify the children with DCD. The prevalence figures worldwide do appear to be around the lower 5% of the population, with an additional 10% in the "at risk" category.

In conclusion, the classifications discussed present an outline of DCD in such a way that a pattern of behaviors are noted, albeit in broad terms. The heterogeneity of children with DCD should be stressed, and despite the entries in ICD-10 (WHO, 1992a, 1992b, 1993) and DSM-IV (APA, 1994), there is still a query as to whether the collection of symptoms described represents a true and distinct syndrome.

THE DIFFERING ABILITIES AND QUALITIES OF CHILDREN WITH DCD

A long-established tradition of comparing and contrasting the differing abilities and qualities of DCD children to age-matched, non-DCD control children currently exists. Individual aspects of DCD dealt with in this way are well-documented: Gubbay (1975a) and Lord and Hulme (1987b), sensory problems; Laszlo et al. (1988), kinesthetic problems; Smyth and Glencross (1986), deficiencies in speed of processing kinesthetic information but not in speed of processing visual information; van Dellen and Geuze (1988) and Rösblad and von Hofsten (1994), slowness but not inaccuracy in the processing of response selection; Dwyer and McKenzie (1994), poor memory for visual patterns over a brief time lapse but not in immediate recall. Mon-Williams et al. (1994) noted that ophthalmic difficulties alone could not explain the difficulty DCD children had with motor control; Geuze and Kalverboer (1987) noted inconsistencies in controlling temporal aspects and imprecision in a finger aiming; Wann (1986, 1987) noted poor handwriting due to inadequate underlying mechanisms for the organization of this skill.

A much less common approach in examining the characteristics of children with DCD is to investigate the differences exhibited within the DCD group. Work by Hoare (1994) acknowledged the heterogeneity of children with DCD and attempted a search for subtypes within the DCD population. Her exploratory study used cluster analysis and confirmed heterogeneity within the DCD group, and she was also able to define five patterns of dysfunction. She concluded that although these children were generally impaired, it is possible to find deficits that generalize across modalities and others that are highly specific. Her work was supported by Wright and Sugden (1996a) who found four clusters of children who, although all experiencing difficulties generally, had specific problem areas, such as manipulating objects at speed or catching objects. In a similar vein, Dewey and Kaplan (1994) identified four groups in their attempt to subtype developmental motor deficits.

PROGNOSIS AND DEVELOPMENTAL FEATURES

For a considerable number of children, the movement difficulties experienced during their early years continue to have an effect into teenage years (Cantell et al., 1994; Geuze & Börger, 1993; Losse et al., 1991). Children with DCD are constantly being observed as they fail to cope with the demands of the environment. Many parents are advised that their children will grow out of the problem and that the physical signs associated with DCD will simply disappear with maturation. The persistence of DCD into later life is a topic that reveals differing and sometimes conflicting results (Cantell et al., 1994). Losse et al. (1991) have shown that many of the difficulties associated with DCD at age 6 are still present at the age of 16. If the difficulties of DCD include social and affective problems, then there is further evidence that DCD lingers into later school life. Relationships are reported, and noted in studies, which demonstrate that having DCD in the early years carries an increased risk of other learning difficulties at school age (Drillien & Drummond, 1983; Gillberg & Gillberg, 1989; Lyytinen & Ahonen, 1989; Silva & Ross, 1980). The children followed in the Losse et al. (1991) study were monitored after 10 years, with almost all of the children who were identified as having motor difficulties soon after beginning primary school still in a similar position as teenagers. Two case studies taken from the Losse et al. (1991) study are considered, to exemplify the difficulties that these children experienced.

Case A: At 5 years old, A had a verbal IQ of 121 and a reading age of 9 years, 6 months. Parental concern had been expressed about A's motor difficulties, and a referral was sought. The parents had been told that she would grow out of the problem. Socially, A was a popular child with a sunny personality, liked by both adults and children. However, she experienced problems climbing stairs, getting dressed and undressed, and in writing correctly. She scored badly on both the Test of Motor Impairment (TOMI; Stott, Moyes, & Henderson, 1984) and on the Neurodevelopmental Test Battery (NDT) at age 5 years.

At age 16, the same modes of assessment were used again, and the extreme clumsiness was still very evident. Her physical education (PE) teachers rated her poorly, and she was known to have other kinds of perceptual motor problems, such as finding her way around school. Her verbal IQ had dropped from a score of 121 to a score of 74, and she had become one of the most problematic children in her class. She was doing very badly in school, had a very low opinion of herself, and was a very unhappy girl.

Case B: In the second case, a 6-year-old boy was coping well academically in school with a verbal IQ of 129. Both his parents and teacher were concerned about his motor problems. At school, the boy had no social difficulties but was noted to be distractible.

When this case was later reviewed, the boy's motor difficulties were still apparent as assessed by the TOMI. He was also rated poorly by his PE teachers. Unlike case A, though, this boy was not in the depressive state that the girl was. However, he too had not made good academic progress but was, in contrast to A, a more well-adjusted child. Though still clumsy, he had many friends and was classified as a pleasant, helpful, and well-behaved pupil. He left school to become a postman.

These case studies, reviewed after such an extended period of time, demonstrate the varied problems encountered by these children and the seemingly detrimental effects of having DCD. However, there are children who do cope with their clumsiness and succeed at school.

Conflicting evidence is reported on development and progression of DCD. Gillberg, Gillberg, and Groth (1989) found that from age 7 to age 13 years, 70% of their original cohort of children with what they called *motor perception dysfunction* (MPD) no longer had this problem. However, in a parallel paper reporting on the same cohort of children, Gillberg and Gillberg (1989) found that 84% of the children with MPD had either behavior or school achievement problems at age 13 years. Losse et al. (1991) found that the children at age 16 continued to have substantial motor difficulties and in addition, had a variety of social, emotional, and educational problems. This is despite showing similar effort in their school work to their peers. The reason behind the different findings of the two studies on the motor competence of the older children may be found in the testing procedures, with a scarcity of validated and well-standardized tests being available for teenage children.

Cantell et al. (1994) report on a longitudinal study of children with DCD at age 5 years and on a follow-up at age 15 years. This study examined the children's motor abilities, educational performances, and some aspects of their social and emotional development. The same children tested at age 5 years were retested at ages 7, 9, and 11 years. During this time, some children moved out of the DCD grouping and, by the age of 15 years, 46% of the original group were classified as the stable DCD group. The other children (named the intermediate group) still performed at lower levels in some movements tasks than their matched controls but were no longer clearly distinguishable from them. Cantell et al. (1994) also found that the intermediate group members were not distinguishable from their controls with regards to aspirations and ambitions. The stable DCD children, however, had lower self-perceptions and took part in fewer social spare-time activities, both physical and nonphysical, than their controls and the intermediate group. Cantell et al. (1994) suggested that social and educational outcomes are poorest for those with the most extreme motor difficulties at 5 years old.

The results of the studies concerned with long-term prognosis of DCD are still somewhat equivocal, although there is a clearer picture developing as the research in the area gets tighter and reexamines previous works. What is evident is that there are children who do not grow out of the condition and that there are children who do literally suffer from the effects of DCD for considerable periods of their childhood, at the very least. The long-term prognosis of DCD is an important question for research to answer, but even if DCD is a temporary difficulty for some children, the anxiety felt by the children and the poor motor skill exhibited are crucial issues to be dealt with at any time.

CONCLUSIONS

In this chapter, we have identified a number of issues that will be elaborated throughout the book. It has been recognized that there is a group of children who evidence disorders of motor function to such a degree that it gives a number of people, often themselves included, cause for concern. The descriptors of this group are becoming more fine grained, and the group has been identified as a distinct childhood syndrome within the specific developmental disorder field. How firm and tight a syndrome the disorder presents is a challenge to the research community. There is now more agreement over terms and characteristics of the disorder, together with a sprinkling of studies examining the nature. However, although great strides have been made, the field is some way behind those in comparable developmental areas, such as language. There are still fundamental issues that require attention, such as the nature of the disorder, its specificity, how it is assessed, and how it develops and progresses.

What does emerge from the research into DCD is a consistent call for intervention and particularly, early intervention. The implications from the Losse et al. (1991) study are that, without additional support for children with DCD as they progress through school, the long-term prognosis is not good. Cantell et al. (1994) believe that treatment of the motor difficulties seen in young children would go a long way to alleviate the problems encountered by children with DCD. In addition, it is also apparent that the earlier a program of management is organized, the greater the positive effect of the intervention, as generalization effects are more likely to occur with young children when the differentiation process has only just started (Schoemaker et al., 1994).

Hoare (1994) further recommends that future studies be developed, whereby children with particular identifiable characteristics and deficits be given intervention based on and related to that characteristic and deficit so that it may be possible to determine if particular teaching methods are more effective with certain groups of DCD children.

2

MOTOR DEVELOPMENT AND CONTROL IN CHILDREN

THE STUDY OF MOTOR DEVELOPMENT

Motor development has had a resurgence of interest during the last decade, not only in describing children's behavior in more detail and with greater accuracy than before but also because new ideas have led to exciting theoretical concepts underlying the explanations of why children develop. The new thinking has come from a number of different sources. First, there have been general steps forward in our concepts about how skills are performed and learned (for a summary, see Latash, 1993; Rosenbaum, 1991; Schmidt, 1988). During the 1970s and to some extent, the 1980s, the study of motor behavior was accomplished by using models from other branches of psychology. There was an enormous increase in literature examining variables that were of a cognitive nature, resulting in books dealing with variables related to the performance and to a lesser extent, the learning of motor skills. More recently, the focus of attention has moved away from models emphasizing the computational or information-processing aspects of motor behavior and toward those that are more dynamic and ecological in nature. These developments have attracted a number of scientists into making a contribution to the development, performance, and learning of motor skills. The theoretical thinking that accompanied the experimental investigation of motor performance and learning had an influence not just on how adults perform but also on children's development and indeed on the field of rehabilitation, whether with children or adults.

The term *development* refers to the process by which children change during the lifespan, and *motor development* involves the adaptive change in children's motor behavior as they move toward different forms of competence. It has generally been related to age, but this is far from a cast-iron index for change because individual differences make any one point in time such a variable measure. Although it has been used as an index of change, age is obviously limited in its predictive power and covaries greatly with maturation and experience. Two different research strategies have been used to investigate the progress and process of development—the cross-sectional and longitudinal designs. A cross-sectional study usually examines children at a particular moment in time and often looks at several age groups simultaneously. A cross-sectional study is relatively quick and easy to do, but it is a moment in time that could have been affected by a number of outside influences not directly connected to the variables being studied. A longitudinal study, on the other hand, follows a group of subjects over a given length of time measuring change. Later in the book, we examine in detail important longitudinal studies of children with DCD that looked at children over a period of time: some from birth to early childhood, others from early childhood through adolescence to early adulthood.

Development is a change in one or more aspects of human behavior—in this case, the motor domain. Motor development has such obvious and dramatic changes, such as the accomplishment of upright locomotion and the growth spurt during puberty, that it is easy to overlook the subtle changes, such as the developing adaptability of reaching and grasping and the emerging ability to react to a moving environment. There are two basic questions in developmental psychology: the first concerns describing change and how children differ at different phases of their lives; the second, asked less frequently, is the causal one involving identifying the agents of these changes.

These two avenues covering motor development do converge on each other, with more accurate descriptions through careful observation of everyday tasks together with more sophisticated experimentation, providing attractive lines of investigation examining the causal agents. Both explanation and description focus on the resolution of a number of issues in the movement domain:

How the child gains control of his or her own body, and how he or she adjusts the control to the demands of a changing environment

When and how new behaviors emerge

How new behaviors are honed and refined to become the effortless skilled behavior we later observe

Why children develop at different rates

During this century, we have chronicled in great detail the changes children make in their progression toward competence in motor development. This detail has enabled us to describe the changes that have taken place in the various phases of a child's development. However, we have been distinctly lacking in providing explanations as to how and why these changes take place. Maturational models, such as those espoused by Gesell (1945/1988) and McGraw (1963), were popular for a long time, and more recently, during the 1970s and early 1980s, models from cognitive theories have been popular, with a tremendous growth in experiments examining internal cognitive explanations and invoking cognitive concepts, such as attention, memory, processing capacity, and feedback. Although this helped popularize motor behavior as a field of study, these models did not provide totally satisfactory explanations for either the performance or the development of motor behavior. More recently, explanations have been offered by those who are promoting dynamic systems as the theoretical underpinnings for how young individuals perform, learn, and change in their motor behavior (Thelen, 1995; Turvey & Fitzpatrick, 1993). A dynamic systems approach does not concentrate on the cognitive processes of the child nor does it invoke pure maturational concepts that gradually unfold with time. It examines the interaction between the demands made by internal constraints, such as body mechanics, and the external environmental requirements.

DESCRIPTION OF CHANGE

Developmental Phases

As with the development of other human abilities, the motor domain is characterized by phases that, although not establishing discrete boundaries of development, provide benchmarks for the descriptive processes. These phases are loosely connected to age, but as we have explained, age is an indicator, not a causal agent, and as such should be treated with caution. For the purpose of using descriptive data for the understanding of the syndrome of DCD, it is convenient to examine phases that involve children from birth to 2 years, 2 to 7 years, 7 years to puberty, and from puberty on.

From the time a baby is born to the age of 2 years, he or she goes through tremendous changes, from an infant who is totally dependent on a carer and who is unable to independently change positions or location, to a toddler who has rudimentary control of posture, can locomote effectively by walking, is starting to run, and has a number of manipulation skills, such as the pincer grip of the thumb and first finger (Keogh & Sugden, 1985). Between the ages of 2 and 7 years, one could make the argument that the child achieves all of the fundamental skills he or she will ever develop naturally. Children do not naturally develop any new skills after this age; they simply refine, combine, extend, play with, and become more proficient in the ones they already possess. Of course, they will learn specific skills, such as skateboarding, but all of the fundamental developmental skills of running, jumping, hopping, climbing, balancing, throwing, catching, striking, riding, skipping, writing, drawing, painting, and so forth are present by roughly 6 years of age. Within this period of development, the child becomes more consistent, more accurate, and better coordinated, with fewer extraneous movements. In addition, force becomes better modulated, and spatial accuracy is quite good when moving in a stable environment. However, when the situation becomes more open and unpredictable with the environment moving, young children react to these changes but in a limited manner. Children in their early school years, although developmentally more mature than younger children, still have difficulty in open situations that are continuous or contain temporal predictions (Keogh & Sugden, 1985).

Between the ages of 7 and puberty, the changes in movement skill development appear to be gradual and progressive, with consistent improvements each year: Children run faster, jump farther, appear stronger, but more important, they are much better at moving in unpredictable environments. In these years, children react faster, develop rules and cognitive strategies, are more accurate at predicting and anticipating, and are better at controlling redundant degrees of freedom, all abilities that enable them to interact better with the environment, thus becoming more proficient in open-movement situations. After 7 years of age, there is a steady increase in the ability to perform closed skills due to the emergence of consistent motor qualities together with a concomitant improvement in more open situations (Bard, Fleury, Carriere, & Belloc, 1981; Keogh & Sugden, 1985; Leavitt, 1979; Shea, Krampitz, Northam, & Ashby, 1982).

From puberty on, our knowledge about the development of skill is much less complete than at earlier ages. This is primarily for two reasons: First, the changes that occur during puberty are usually associated with maximum-performance variables, such as size, speed, strength, and stamina, and skill tasks tend to be contaminated by these variables. Put another way, by the age of 14 or 15, many motor tasks are either accomplished by the vast majority of children or involve strength and speed to such a degree that skill is being overridden. Second, much of what we know about later motor development is dependent on the experiences of children who tend to practice fewer motor skills but concentrate on them for recreational, leisure, or competitive purposes.

There are a number of ways in which the motor development in children can be illustrated so that a behavioral description and picture of the process can be obtained. We have chosen to take the two actions of manual skills and locomotor skills that are common across cultures and ages and involve numerous subcomponents. These are two skills that are usually involved when we are describing children's movement difficulties. Children with DCD often show difficulties related to locomotion—running, jumping, and playing games—and manual functions are often delayed, awkward, and inappropriate. An examination of the normal developmental progressions helps us monitor change and can provide guidelines for intervention.

Manual Skills

Manual control describes the actions of reaching, grasping, and manipulating, where the hands and arms work in unison to control various objects. From very early in life, we use manual skills, and by the end of the first year, infants are proficient in a number of reaching and grasping and manipulation activities. Throughout life, much of our everyday activity involves skilled manual behavior.

A number of landmarks are present in a baby's early life, which includes picking up an object such as a cube at around 3 or 4 months. At 5 or 6 months, children move to thumb opposition, in which the thumb opposes the fingers during the grasping, whereas the grasping of smaller objects around 9 months requires the opposition of the thumb with one finger, called the *neat pincer grasp*. From this point on, the precision grip has been achieved, and digital control of the object is now possible, enabling various forms of manipulation to start (Corbetta & Mounoud, 1990; Jeannerod, 1988; Keogh & Sugden, 1985).

Underlying processes, such as the use of vision, are common threads across reaching and grasping at all ages. The use of visual control during reaching and grasping starts with hand regard at about 2 to 3 months of age and a crude reach and touch by 3 or 4 months, and by 6 months of age, babies can position their hands accurately and easily. Of great interest with respect to classification of skills into those movements for self and those movements with others is the work of Von Hofsten (1980) who showed in a series of elegant studies that by around 4 months of age, babies can track moving objects and can move a hand ahead of the object to intercept it. Von Hofsten not only showed that babies were much more competent than previously thought but also showed different ways of examining reaching and grasping. From the age of 4 months, babies start to anticipate moving objects, and at this age, the visual-motor aspects seem to be better developed than the motor control parts, with the control of the arm improving significantly by 6 months with more refinements by 9 months. The infant can look at the object and move the hand accordingly, thus establishing at an early age the coordination between what the eye sees and what the hand does (Corbetta & Mounoud, 1990; Jeannerod, 1988; Keogh & Sugden, 1985).

A further progression in babies' manual skills is the differentiation between reaching and grasping. At first, reaching and grasping is a single unitary movement performed with the total body so that both trunk and arm moves toward the object. By 4 or 5 months of age, the reach is becoming distinct from the grasp, and this separation appears to be complete by 6 months of age when babies will not grasp in a virtual-object situation. The accuracy of babies reaching and grasping also increases from about 40% correct trials at 3 months of age to very few misses at 4 or 5 months.

The research work done with babies is important not only because it provides richer information on babies' functioning but because many of the processes that are examined occur in later childhood and with different tasks. For example, the interception studies of Von Hofsten (1980) with babies have parallels with studies performed on older children (Bard, Fleury, & Gagnon, 1990; Dorfman, 1977; Shea et al., 1982; Wade 1980).

There are numerous ways in which children develop their manual control as they get older, and it is difficult to systematically chronicle the changes because of the different functions hands perform. However, it is possible to examine certain tasks in isolation and relate these to the structure we have described earlier.

Self help skills have been chronicled extensively, and children with DCD are often reported to have difficulties. It is also an area showing great variation in normative data on tasks such as dressing because of the difference in the tasks that are presented and in the different conditions in which the children are expected to dress. Dressing is a good example, with putting on a garment such as a sweater requiring the child to match the garment to the appropriate body parts in an appropriate spatial relationship, such as back and front, top and bottom. It is usually a bimanual task and requires very little manual dexterity. Putting on shoes is very different in that the spatial orientation demand is not high, although left-right is often a problem, but it is a difficult task requiring dexterity to be able to tie shoe laces. This task is made more difficult by the laces being free and not firm and having no definitive target as support. Fastening buttons is different again in that it requires great dexterity, but there is a target (button hole) and the button itself is firm and cannot take on another shape, unlike a lace. On the other hand, many buttons have to be done without vision, relying on kinesthetic and tactile information, and occasionally (cuffs) have to be fastened with one hand. Children with

DCD, particularly those described as dyspraxic, very often show difficulties on this type of task where strategic planning is involved.

After the age of 2, children start to develop representational skills, and again, when parents, teachers, and professionals are describing children with DCD, they very often refer to handwriting that is illegible or terribly slow. We know that handwriting can be improved, but we often forget that speed of writing is also important, particularly in the secondary school where the ability to take notes quickly is valued. This is a simple example of how difficulties in early childhood have greater long-term effects than at first envisaged. Simple tasks, such as the nature of the grasp and posture, show great variety within children.

From an early age, children engage in crude scribbling, with random marks made with no apparent plan; lines, crosses, squares, and more exact geometrical figures are presented; coloring in becomes more accurate. These skills have been studied in great detail, with Kellogg and O'Dell (1969), for example, noting about 20 substeps in the development of scribbling. Enclosing space, loops, circles, and squared-off circles all emerge. By the age of 5, children's drawings of rectangles, circles, and squares are clearly separable, but not many can draw a good triangle at that age. When printing letters, 4-year-olds tend to scatter them on the page with little regard for a stable baseline; by 5, most children are able to print their first names, and by 6, children can print first and last name, the numbers from 1 to 10, and the letters of the alphabet.

The use of visual information to intercept moving objects is clearly used as early as 4 months of age, but there are also changes in early childhood as the tasks become more complex, and the results seen in babies are repeated later in early childhood. On any new task, vision is often not used in the initial stages for the ongoing control of the movement; the action is usually ballistic in nature with some kind of program determining the beginning and end points of the movement. As vision is brought in, it does not aid the performance of the movement in the first instance and in some cases, acts as a disruptive influence (Hay, 1979, 1990). However, as children develop, they are better able to use visual information in a flexible manner, choosing to use it when necessary.

We use our hands and arms in a myriad of ways every day, and this starts from the day we are born. There are natural progressions in the performance of age-appropriate tasks, noting that in general as children develop with age, so the performance of these tasks improves. In addition, it is clear that the manner in which these tasks are performed also changes with development, with variables such as the use and importance of vision recurring throughout the developmental period. So when a child is identified as having DCD, at one level, we can say the child is having difficulty performing age-appropriate skills (such as poor handwriting), is not involved in peer games in the playground, has difficulty with some self help skills, or cannot play ball games. At another level, we can ask about some of the underlying variables that affect the performance of such skills and investigate whether the problem is more of a motor control issue with the actual hand movement being devoid of dexterity, such as in movements for self where the child has ample time to accomplish the task. Furthermore, we can examine variables such as visual information and determine whether it is being used in an appropriate manner or determine whether anticipatory mechanisms appeared to be giving cause for concern when moving with others. A final explanation occurs when the child is having difficulty representing what he or she has seen as writing and drawing. Ecological psychologists dealing with dynamic systems would argue that action and perception are inseparable in the demands of the task, and one of the issues that will recur later is whether, when a difficulty is found, the approach is to break it down into some component subsections, such as in anticipation tasks, or whether the action-perception link is kept alive and whole in any practice. The development of manual skills is a crucial aspect of a child's overall development, and problems in this area—handwriting, reaching and grasping, and manipulation—are all seen as serious when describing a child's functioning.

Locomotor Skills

Locomotion, including posture, is a movement problem that the young infant must resolve. It includes control of the whole body for movements involving self control and those involving moving others. Posture or general body position must be controlled to allow other movements to take place. Developmental milestones are well-described, and in posture, the first major landmark occurs around 2 months, when the baby can keep the head steady without support while being held. The second landmark occurs when the baby can sit upright without support, generally occurring around 5 months of age. The third landmark is when the baby can achieve and maintain a standing position. They can pull to a standing position at 7 or 8 months and stand alone at 10 or 11 months, ready for walking. By this age, children can adopt a variety of postures and move skillfully between them, thus solving the problem of maintaining one position and moving to a new one. Locomotor activities and achievements are progressing at the same time and are often dependent on postural developments.

During the first 6 months, babies are rarely mobile with respect to locomotion. But at that age, they begin rolling over from supine to prone position and back again. At around 7 months, they start to move forward in a prone position and show various forms of this locomotion. One form is crawling, where the arms pull and legs push and the baby is close to the floor. When babies are in all-fours positions, they are creeping. Some babies do neither and move by sitting and scooting on their bottoms. One of the major landmark achievements is walking alone, which occurs at around 12 months of age, although depending on which study is taken, the mean age can be anything from 11 to 14 months.

From the age of around 2 years to about 6, the child acquires a tremendous repertoire of locomotor skills. As walking proficiency is gained, the child begins to adopt a narrower and more rhythmic gait with the feet now pointing straight ahead and the heel of one foot moving ahead of the toe of the other in stride pattern. At first, the child still has to monitor walking through vision, but as the walking becomes more automatic, the visual monitoring disappears. From the age of 18 months on, the child shows some kind of run, but it is usually between the ages of 2 and 3 that a genuine run appears—genuine in that both feet are off the ground at the same time. By 4 and 5 years of age, the running is much improved with reciprocal arm action being present. At this time, it is also possible for children to give a maximum performance.

Jumping again starts at the end of the child's second year and by 2 years, will show a 2-foot take-off jump. The arm action accompanying the legs goes through stages of little use, to swinging in the opposite, that is, least efficient, direction, to one where the arms and legs move together as though one single functional unit. By 5 years of age, children can jump around 3 feet in distance and about 1 foot in height. By the age of $3\frac{1}{2}$, most children can hop one to three times on their preferred foot, and by 5 or 6 years of age, the number of hops is extended to around 10. Rhythmic hopping is a more difficult activity, and by 5, only around 10% of boys can execute a simple two-two rhythm moving from one foot to the other. A slightly higher percentage of girls can accomplish this task. By 5, most can hop 50 feet in around 10 seconds, with girls slightly faster than the boys. Variations on hopping include skipping and galloping and are often not achieved until 6 years of age. At 5, only about 20% can skip with any degree of proficiency (Keogh & Sugden, 1985).

From the age of 6 or 7 onward, the child is refining locomotor skills and using them in play-game situations and is also becoming much more proficient at dealing with open, unpredictable situations. Leavitt (1979) measured the speed of boys and young men when ice skating through a 50-foot course with cones to negotiate. The subjects performed faster with increasing age, but there was only a drop in time from around 8 seconds at 6 years of age to just below 5 seconds at 20 years of age. However, when they were asked to control a puck at the same time as skating for speed, the time dropped from 16 seconds at 6 years to 5 seconds at 20 years, with the major decrease coming between 6 and 14 years of age and little improvement after that.

During this period of time, the child is also engaged in tasks that require maximal performance, and we have strong data showing age trends on a variety of activities. In the standing long jump, there is little difference between boys and girls before the age of 11 or 12, but the boys continue to improve during that period with the girls plateauing. A similar picture is portrayed when running speed is considered, with few differences between the sexes up to 12, but the girls then level off, whereas the boys continue to improve. At that age, the girls are probably through the pubertal period, whereas the boys are just starting, and the changes that take place during puberty do so for a longer period of time and to a greater intensity in boys.

EXPLANATION OF CHANGE

Historical Perspective

With development, motor behavior becomes more differentiated, increasing the diversity and complexity of an individual's repertoire. Major questions surround how a child changes from a state of limited actions to one that involves a rich vocabulary of skills readily adaptable to numerous situations. A historical view of the study of motor development includes the domination by two approaches over the past 50 years. Chronologically, the first involved maturational concepts as espoused by individuals such as Gesell (1945) and McGraw (1963), who gained their ideas from meticulous longitudinal observation of children and used as an explanation the natural biological unfolding of behaviors. The second approach became known as information processing, coming from the influential cognitive psychology camps in the late 1960s and 1970s. In the information-processing approach, children were viewed as systems that processed information, and various stages of processing were identified for the input, transformation, storage, and production. This approach differed greatly from the maturational hypothesis, with a much greater emphasis on the interaction of the individual and the environment. However, it was still concerned with within-child variables to a great extent and regarded motor development as being heavily reliant on the build up and construction of cognitive structures, such as subroutines, motor programs, capacities, memory strategies, and so forth.

Maturation

Although criticizing the maturation approach, Thelen (1995) still applauds the detail that early pioneers of movement observation presented, noting that some of them were also theorists. Gesell (1945) and McGraw (1963), noting the regularity with which children passed through motor milestones, assigned explanations for these changes to maturational processes in the infant's nervous system. To these investigators, motor development was a series of naturally unfolding structures in the nervous system driven internally, although Manoel and Connolly (1997) do note that McGraw (1946, 1963) recognized that the structure-function relationship could be bidirectional. This argument is also taken up by Lockman and Thelen (1993) who suggest that it is pertinent to move away from the nature debate or whether we can ascribe a particular behavior to a certain part of the nervous system, but "what goes on in the nervous system must be reflected in behavior, but it is equally true that what goes on as behavior must sculpt and mold the nervous system" (p. 958).

Thelen (1995) believes that this maturational concept was then extended to other fields of development, notably in cognitive behavior and the work of Piaget, and thus became the standard by which developmental ideas and theories were constructed. One outcome of the naturists' views of motor development and indeed of the cognitive explanations was that motor development was viewed as a tool of developmental assessment rather than a suitable topic for process-oriented research. The emphasis of study was not always the motor functioning of the child, with emphasis not on motor behaviors per se but on other developmental outcomes or indicators of cognitive processing.

Information Processing

The information-processing approach did not emerge in response to questions concerning motor behavior but, once applied to some fundamental issues, became the dominant paradigm in the 1960s and 1970s. Although the approach as a holistic theoretical explanation of motor behavior is now not favored, microcomponents of the approach are still prevalent in many studies. Central tenets of the approach involved, first, the process of action being broken down into a number of subcomponents and second, an emphasis on central representation (cortical) of these subcomponents. Thus, the study of action involved an in-depth look at sensory attention mechanisms, at speed of decisions in the form of reaction times, storage, interference, retention and retrieval in memory, feedback, and concepts such as motor programs. Many of these were brought together in schema theory (Schmidt, 1975), which involved the development of a generalized motor program to fit a certain class of movements. Learning took place by the individual refining the motor program by a constant comparison of the movement with previous actions within the same class of events, thus strengthening the motor schema. It was an extension of Bartlett's (1932) earlier work on schema and did suggest answers to the question as to how the system produces novel movements. Over the past 20 years, schema theory has probably been investigated as much as any central concept in the motor domain.

The influence of the information-processing approach has been huge. It has allowed researchers to investigate more closely and clearly the processes involved in motor behavior. It has generated masses of data describing and explaining motor actions, and most of all, it has generated debate by involving a larger and more diverse group of researchers examining the motor domain. From this group, criticism of the approach has also emerged, and new ways of examining motor actions leading to new explanations of motor development have been proposed.

DYNAMIC SYSTEMS AND ECOLOGICAL PSYCHOLOGY

Background

The work of the Russian physiologist Nicolai Bernstein (1967) in his influential book, *The Coordination and Regulation of Movement,* has had an enormous effect on the theoretical thinking of researchers in the motor control area, which in turn has influenced our thinking about development. Bernstein was the first one to examine in detail the problems of the brain-to-behavior causal link. He examined the concept of coordination asking how an organism with many muscles and millions of nerves can coordinate these into smooth purposeful movement without involving some homunculus that had the program already stored. This became known as the "degrees of freedom" problem, whereby the question of how the variables that are free to vary in any movement are controlled. A supplementary question for developmentalists concerns the progression of the control of these variables through the lifespan of an individual.

Bernstein (1967) rejected the notion of a one-to-one correspondence between the firing of motoneurons and particular movement patterns. Purposeful movements can come about from a variety of underlying muscular contractions. The analogy with language and the underlying meaning being addressed by a variety of surface grammatical structures is reasonably accurate. Goal-directed actions, such as picking up a cup, can be accomplished in a variety of different ways, using different hands, trajectory, grip to a target of different sizes, at different heights, and so forth. Depending where the arm is in space, the same muscle contractions can have different consequences for the movement. Bernstein noted that because of this, the movements are not programmed in detail but are planned at an abstract level and then are honed and refined by the demands of the task. The term *softly assembled* has been used to describe this process, noting that it facilitates great flexibility in responding to a continually changing environment. In addition, Bernstein notes the biomechanical constraints that are influential in movements, describing the elastic qualities of muscles and the anatomical configuration of joints that enable the limbs to have springlike qualities, meaning that a limb when stretched and released will oscillate on a regular trajectory until it comes to rest at a given equilibrium point. These observations cast doubt on any explanation that relies heavily on simple nervous system maturation as the process by which infants develop motor coordination. The ideas of Bernstein have been elaborated by a number of researchers, such as Kelso, Kugler, Thelen, and Turvey (Kelso & Tuller, 1984; Kugler & Turvey, 1987; Thelen, 1995; Turvey, 1990), and have been an influential force behind ideas that have come to be labeled as a dynamic systems approach.

Stability and Instability

In the models proposed by Thelen, Kugler, Kelso, and Turvey (Kelso & Tuller, 1984; Kugler & Turvey, 1987; Thelen, 1995; Turvey, 1990), development is dynamic, and patterns of movement emerge from particular constraints with preferred patterns of behavior that are self-organized. The dynamic systems explanation of development emphasizes that the infant explores and finds solutions to new environmental demands. It is not simply a matter of maturation driving the infant; it is the task that motivates the infant interacting with the child's resources and producing the driving force for change. These preferred patterns or attractors are those that the system wants to perform and can only move out of them with difficulty. When the system is stable, it is performing these preferred patterns, and change is noted by bringing in instability. Thus, change is brought about by a disruption of the stable position, and the agents of instability are many and varied, such as growth, biochemical factors, biomechanical factors, experience, practice, or environmental conditions. A number of authors have used Waddington's (1957) epigenetic landscape to reflect as a model of how development takes place (Connolly, 1986; Thelen, 1995). Thelen notes that when a ball runs through this landscape, a deep, narrow fissure is characterized by stability but also a limited number of options, whereas when the landscape is smooth, without fissures, the system is inherently unstable with lots of options. Thelen believes that instability is necessary for any flexible system to select adaptive activities and is therefore necessary for change and development.

The work of Clark and Phillips (1993) examined stability and instability using a dynamic systems strategy by analyzing collective variables for the leg's segmental motion over a 1-year period in 5 infants. They examined the notion of instability and how long it lasted and what happened when the system was perturbed. The infant showed the same dynamic solutions to walking as the adult, but the solution was unstable, with the infant at first refusing to walk when a weight was attached to the ankle, and yet within 3 months, the system had stabilized. Similarly, this also occurred with the thigh and shank limit cycle systems, with an adultlike pattern appearing after 3 months of walking. There was a period of instability at the onset of a new movement, and after a period of time, this stabilized, confirming predictions made by a dynamic systems approach.

The nervous system is dynamic and self-organizing, and repeated cycles of perception and action facilitate new forms of behavior without having to resort to explanations involving mental or genetic structures; it is a move away from the idea that internal mechanisms, such as genes, programs, and cognitive structures, contain the blueprint for behavioral change. Tasks and internal mechanisms are dynamic in their working at different times and on different scales. Even mental structures are activity dependent in the same ways as children develop reaching and grasping by repeated attempts at the task. The question then becomes how do these different parts "cooperate" to produce stability or engender change. If these factors can be discovered, then we may be able to move the system into new unstable forms, offering diversity and flexibility in adapting to new demands. How can we disrupt the current stable dynamics to foster new and better solutions?

Sporns and Edelman (1993) suggest that a baby's spontaneous exploratory movements are the key elements in motor development, with sensory and motor neurons becoming increasingly linked as a motor problem is consistently solved. There are a number of levels of how sensorimotor coordination is attained—at the brain level, the perceptual motor apparatus level, and the level of the organism's behavior. Children interact with their environments primarily through skilled actions, and through these, they are able to solve problems set by the environment and devise new interactions. Thus, it is a fundamentally important issue to know how skilled actions are organized.

Movements are necessary for action, but they are not sufficient explanation (Connolly, 1975). Skilled actions that develop tend to be relatively permanent and become more complex and diverse. At times during development, a stable structure is acquired that is then modified and reorganized into a new one. This has rarely been studied, yet this continuous reorganization is a fundamental requirement to meet the increasingly complex environmental demands. As a child develops motor skills, such as reaching and grasping or walking, there is a succession of changes in which the action (e.g., walking) becomes more refined. These changes illustrate a movement from a state of low organization or relative disorder to a state of higher organization or greater order and stability (Kugler, 1986).

Selection and Motor Development

Earlier, we introduced the concept of coordinative structure or synergy to explain how the many degrees of freedom in any particular movement can be controlled. Questions arise as to the nature of these and how they originate and develop. Some synergies or coordinative structures, because they are associated with certain muscle groups, can at least partially be defined by morphology and anatomy. On the other hand, some are clearly related to a given task and capture the topological rather than the metric features of the movement. Most synergies for everyday movements emerge early in life, such as those for walking and reaching; however, there is still the issue of the selection of synergies for a given situation. Many of the defining characteristics of synergies such as timing invariance have been found over a wide range of tasks (see Schmidt, 1988).

Sporns and Edelman (1993) propose a theory of selection as providing the basis for motor development, noting that development must involve a generation of basic movement repertoires for richness and variability of movement; it must involve the ability to sense the effect of the movement on the environment, thereby providing an adaptive value to the movement; and it must include a mechanism by which those movements are selected that satisfy both environmental demands and internal constraints. Thus, selection is a key aspect of change in motor coordination, and successive selection will involve progressive modification of a given movement repertoire, and a change in the biomechanics or environmental demand will also drive selection and lead to more adaptive coordination. This alleviates the need to solve a problem by computational or processing means and replaces it with the organism selecting purposeful movements-synergies from a wide range that have adaptively developed to solve environmental and mechanical problems.

There is no need to specifically make computations containing dynamic and kinematic terms; the organism discovers possible solutions that satisfy the task demands and the internal constraints. The variability notion, such an issue for information-processing explanations, becomes a necessary condition, with the movement being selected as a whole pattern and not broken down into component parts. There is little evidence that the nervous system computes desired trajectories and makes micro comparisons between actual and desired outcomes.

Questions arise in development as to how a child changes from a stage of a limited set of actions to one in which diverse and complex actions are made in a set of environments. Similar questions are asked about how a novice performer becomes skilled over a period of time. In dynamic systems, there is a move from a situation where degrees of freedom are constrained, through to a relaxing of degrees of freedom, to exploiting active and passive forces (e.g., gravity and inertial forces) to improve performance (Vereijken, Whiting, & Beek, 1992). An example of this is from the work of Clark and Phillips (1993) who argue that in learning to walk, the infant is attracted to an unstable weak dynamic solution (freezing degrees of freedom) that is then stabilized through experience, allowing adaptive behavior to develop (freeing degrees of freedom).

Thus, in a dynamic systems approach, great emphasis is placed on the role of exploration when explaining changes in skilled actions, and development is seen as exploring the dynamics of action leading to some stable state. It follows that exploration leads to selection that in turn leads to optimal solutions to environmental problems constrained by internal qualities. This exploration and selection is first available in the reflexive and spontaneous movements of the young infant. However, how this selection is ultimately linked with the emergence, breakdown, and reorganization of structures necessary for skilled behavior remains a basic issue.

CONCLUSIONS

The two issues addressed in this chapter of description and explanation of motor development provide framework and background for our analysis of DCDs. The descriptions enable us to examine expectations in children's development, and whereas caution is recommended, particularly when only a few behaviors are observed, they do provide us with benchmarks that are useful in our identification and assessment procedures. We have taken the two areas of locomotion and manual skills to show as examples of changes as children develop. Each one of these can be broken down into much finer detail and analyzed accordingly.

Explaining motor development goes beyond description and involves an examination of the processes that drive the changes seen in children. The maturational and information-processing approaches to motor development have dominated our explanations of change, and the latter has provided us with a number of fruitful ways in which to examine and remediate motor difficulties. The motor act in children with difficulties has been broken down into its component parts, such as sensory input, attention, memory, and motor programs, and remediation has been specifically directed toward these. Descriptions of what children need to know as well as do when performing a motor skill have led directly to the development of intervention programs. More recently, both maturation and information-processing explanations have been challenged in new and exciting ways. A dynamic systems approach to explaining motor behavior in general involves selection based on both internal and environmental constraints, and it logically follows that differences in development we observe, and in particular those differences that become profound and disabling, are also the results of these internal and external constraints. The carryover from explanations of motor development using a dynamic systems approach to work with children showing coordination disorders is in its infancy. However, it does appear to be a particularly attractive proposition for analyzing the nature of coordination disorders, the assessment in context, and for developing principles into practice for intervention. Ulrich (1997) notes that the essence of causality from a dynamic systems approach is behavior being the result of multiple subsystems that change over time in a nonlinear fashion. These multiple subsystems are complex, and it is unlikely that they can be studied in any unidimensional manner. Our knowledge is presently limited, but the approach offers such exciting opportunities through a diversity of paradigms examining real-life actions rather than fragments of movements.

3

IDENTIFICATION AND ASSESSMENT

Methods of identification and assessment are inextricably linked to the nature and characteristics of any disorder and indeed, often determine what the central features are. In the case of motor disorders, a number of formal and informal modes of identification have been employed, and when different methods have been compared, there is usually less than complete agreement (Keogh et al., 1979; Maeland, 1992). We should not be surprised by this because these types of motor disorders are often assessed in a functional manner, and function can be assessed by different people in a range of contexts using a variety of instruments with differing purposes. For example, a parent may first notice that a child is not achieving various motor milestones in the same way as siblings or friends; teachers may notice that a child is having difficulty handling puzzles, zippers, and other manipulative tasks and as the child starts to write and draw, notices that the child has difficulty forming letters and in catching a ball during PE. A physiotherapist, on the other hand, may observe the child and concentrate on the sensory integrative behaviors: The difficulty is viewed at a different, almost causal, level rather than the purely functional. A pediatrician may give a neurological examination to provide backing to some of the mentioned observations. The child can be assessed in the home situation, in school within the classroom, on the playing field, or in a more informal social setting in the playground. Keogh et al. (1979) identified children with movement difficulties by a standardized test, by asking teachers and then by observing children in the school situation. The results were disappointingly varied, with few children being identified across all situations. Maeland (1992) compared incidence rates across countries using different tests and found that the tests identify the same number of children, around 5% to 6%, but different sets of children. However, although there is no so-called gold standard of assessment, we do believe we have sufficient information and techniques to be able to make reasonably accurate identification and assessment leading to diagnosis and intervention. We also believe that a number of children have pervasive difficulties that go across contexts, whereas the difficulties of others are seen more often in certain environmental situations. In this chapter, we aim to raise a number of issues concerning assessment and then present an overview of some assessment instruments. These instruments are a selection of certain types of test rather than a comprehensive survey of what is available.

A major concern when examining assessment processes and instruments is why the test is being used and for what purpose will the results be used. Very often, motor behavior is assessed as part of a larger battery of overall development. These general tests of development give a professional an overview of a child's profile of abilities, and these tests are particularly useful when determining placement in schools or classes. But for a more detailed examination of the motor behavior, tests that directly address motor aspects of a child's functioning are required. The aims of some instruments are not solely motor behavior, and although this is appropriate, we are also of the opinion that motor behavior in general and motor difficulties in particular are, in their own right, an important part of a child's functioning, and although they may be correlated with other aspects of a child's behavior, this is a secondary concern of ours.

RELIABILITY AND VALIDITY

The twin concepts of reliability and validity are the cornerstone of formal assessment procedures for any disorder, and this is equally true with motor difficulties. Reliability of assessment refers to the consistency or freedom from any systematic measurement error. Reliability over time is one type; if an assessment instrument is repeatedly given over a relatively short period of time with no specific intervention in between, similar patterns of scores should be obtained. However, there are many gray areas here. For example, if the instrument is task-oriented and given to the child, the child may remember the items and become more familiar with them and indeed, could practice them. Similarly, if the instrument is a checklist type, the observer could remember how it was scored a previous time, and this could bias the ongoing score. A second and crucial reliability measure is one of interobserver reliability. If the test is a normative-based, standardized test, different trained testers should obtain very similar results from a given child. Likewise, if the test is a checklist type with given categories of motor behavior with a formal scoring procedure, different observers should be able to obtain similar scores both overall and within any individual sections of a test, provided they are observing at the same time. If a checklist is being used in a variety of situations by more than one observer, then the same behaviors may be scored differently because of the context variations. Last, a consistent instrument should be internally reliable, with each item specifically measuring a given domain of functioning without being influenced by other areas.

Like reliability, validity has a number of facets and can be examined in various ways. At its simplest, validity is the ability of the test to assess what it is meant to assess. If motor performance is the goal, does the instrument actually assess motor performance as defined by a number of criteria? So-called *face validity* is often used as a criteria for validity; does the test "look right?" This is regularly used, but it is in fact a rather crude measure and is susceptible to the idiosyncratic interpretations of individual professionals. *Construct validity* examines the theoretical proposals behind the construction of any test. If a test of motor performance is divided into four subcomponents of balance, locomotion, manipulation, and ball skills, what is the rationale behind this division? How strong is the theoretical literature supporting this as covering the range of motor performance? The significant point about construct validity is its emphasis on the theoretical foundations of the test, the testing of the proportion of variance accounted for by the various components, and the testing of hypothesized relations between the various components. *Content validity* refers to the representativeness of the test; once the construct validity of the test has been confirmed, content validity follows on by an examination of whether the test's subcomponents are representative of the domain in question. One can examine each item for relevance to the domain in question and in particular, for ambiguity and relationship and overlap to other items on the test. It is basically judgmental, with each item being examined for its representation and for its presumed relevance to the property being measured. In many cases, competent judges must be employed to adequately achieve this task. However, both construct and content validity could be said to be addressing the concept of the test and are extensions of what we have labeled as the rather crude face validity.

A test is often judged for its predictive or concurrent validity. Does the instrument predict accurately other independent measures of the same domain? Does a standardized test correlate with a well-established observational instrument and vice versa. These are seen as different and separate from construct and content but could also be seen as operationalizing them. If one compares a test with an outside criterion, some differences will be often obtained and indeed are deemed desirable because of different contexts and situations.

APPROACHES TO IDENTIFICATION AND ASSESSMENT

It is not surprising that we have a number of different approaches to identifying children with movement disorders because these children do not form an homogeneous group (Hoare, 1994; Wright & Sugden, 1996a). A critical examination of the various subgroups within the movement disorder domain is still in its infancy, and it is difficult to specify precisely what the subgroups are. It is an almost circular process; Wright and Sugden (1996a) note the various subgroups they identify, but these subgroups are a direct function of the methods of assessment. Only when this procedure has been completed a number of times across population groups with different tasks and some form of metaanalysis has been employed can we arrive at any definitive subgrouping.

A critical analysis of the types of assessment instruments and methodology was undertaken by Henderson (1987). She notes the heterogeneity of this group of children, highlighting that this is just one of a number of variable aspects of motor disorders. Variability exists in the range of difficulties, in the severity, and in the development of such problems over time. There is, in addition, variation found in concomitant impairment of other aspects of behaviors, leading some researchers to propose the existence of the clumsy child syndrome (Gubbay, 1975b).

In her review of assessment types, Henderson (1987) divides tests into those that she labels traditional and have formed the basis of assessments by psychologists, pediatricians, therapists, and teachers, and those she labels alternative and have emerged as a result of the criticisms aimed at the traditional approaches. She further divides the traditional approaches into descriptive tests, diagnostic tests, and neurodevelopmental test batteries. Descriptive tests usually are aimed at assessing functional performance in everyday actions, recording what the child can or cannot do, and usually produce a quantitative measure of the child's performance. These tests have the further characteristic of using chronological age as the yardstick against which performance is judged, with composite scores being used in a normative manner to compare child against child. Some of these tests use the total range of children, whereas others are aiming only to identify those children experiencing difficulties. These tests range from relatively simple checklists to comprehensive batteries involving standardized equipment. Henderson notes the criticisms of these tests that point to the viability of using chronological age as a yardstick and the relative crudity of the scoring system. However, she also notes their usefulness in confirming parent or teacher views of the child and for providing the starting point for future action.

Diagnostic tests are usually constructed by educators and therapists and are often devised with motives other than an examination of pure motor behaviors. Specifically, the professionals involved with this kind of test are interested in the relationship between perceptual-motor performance and academic achievement, particularly reading. At a theoretical level, reading is thought to be a sensory-perceptual experience, and this could be governed by perceptual motor abilities. Any delay in this perceptual-motor experience could have effects that lead to learning problems. At a practical level, these tests led to various forms of intervention that had the direct aim of improving perceptual-motor performance but had the more indirect goal of improving academic achievement through the improved perceptual-motor performance. These theoretical formulations were conceived in the 1960s and proved very popular among professionals, parents, and the press. Typical of these programs and their accompanying instruments were those of Ayres (1972), Barsch (1967), Frostig and Maslow (1973), Getman (1965), and Kephart (1960). Although they were popular, they were not without their critics, with Cratty (1981) being a constant and rigorous critic. More recently, Kavale and Forness (1995) more or less confirm Cratty's (1981) views by noting that empirical evidence and support for the link between perceptual-motor programs and academic performance was not strong. The assessment instruments that these individuals proposed did include items that were more perceptual than motor in nature because of the proposed links between perception and learning difficulties.

The difference between descriptive and diagnostic tests is often not clear-cut; sometimes, the diagnostic tests will include items with a more perceptual emphasis, but this is also true of many descriptive tests, such as bead threading and drawing between lines, which are items on tests such as the Movement ABC (Henderson & Sugden, 1992). Henderson's (1987) conclusions on this are probably the most sensible guidelines. She notes that a distinction has to be drawn about the aims of the test. Those that purport to assess perceptual-motor performance with a view to diagnosing academic achievement difficulties should be distinguished from those that are aiming to assess motor performance per se.

Henderson's (1987) third type of traditional test is the neurodevelopmental examination almost exclusively used by the medical profession, who have historically played an important role in the identification, assessment, and intervention of children with movement disorders. Often, this has moved neurologists down the road of a concept involving minimal brain damage, usually diagnosed on the basis of a neurodevelopmental test. Minimal brain dysfunction, or damage, is a concept with a checkered history over the past 30 years. It is usually diagnosed on the basis of behavioral tests that although showing no actual brain damage, point to some neurological dysfunction being present. For clinicians, it has been a popular concept to use in their diagnosis, whereas for some researchers, there is lack of evidence for the use of such a term. However, the term and concept are used, and studies such as the Collaborative Perinatal Project (Nichols & Chen, 1981) select a number of test items that best represent minimal brain damage symptoms. In their case, 26 test items were used, including 7 behavioral observations, 6 cognitive and perceptual-motor tests, 3 academic tasks, and 10 neurological tests. In studies such as the Collaborative Perinatal Project, there is a confusing mix between neurological tests and others that are more or less related.

Even in neurological tests, there is considerable range in content from the impressionistic to the more quantitative signs, with issues such as reliability and validity rarely being addressed in a comprehensive manner. Henderson (1987) notes that at the heart of the neurological examination is the so-called soft sign, which indicates that there is neurological dysfunction but for which no underlying neurological disorder can be found. Again, variability in the behaviors under this heading make it difficult to come to some agreement on an overall profile, particularly if scores are pooled from the various items. Henderson (1987) summarizes these tests by noting that from a research point of view, they are useful in the exploration that examines the relationship between functional behaviors and their neural correlates.

Henderson (1987) concludes her paper by noting that the general dissatisfaction some professionals have with traditional types of tests has led them to explore more alternative methods. She outlines two types of alternative assessments—documenting how actions are performed, which includes verbal descriptions and biomechanical analysis, and analyzing component processes. The first type involves not just examining the product of any movement but describing the actual movement itself. Verbal descriptions are an obvious way and require observation usually guided by verbal descriptions of a prescribed pattern. These descriptions usually require the observer to judge whether or not the child's movements conform to a standard criterion, which has criteria obtained from an analysis of a mature action (McClenaghan & Gallahue, 1978; Ulrich, 1985). A major problem with these is that the observer is required to have some competence, and thus, they have limitations for individuals with little or no experience. Biomechanical or motion analysis using kinematic instruments can provide minutely detailed quantitative analysis of such variables as accelerations, velocities, angles of joints, and relationships between joints. Recent developments in this area can provide three-dimensional information on how muscles and joints are coordinated to provide skillful or not so skillful actions. At the moment, it is primarily being used for research purposes, but as more motion analysis systems are being made available, the translation of this work by physiotherapists and related professionals could be a challenge and a way ahead. Last, Henderson (1987) describes what she calls *analysis of component processes,* which involves an information-processing explanation of motor behavior, allowing us to break down any action into its component parts. Thus, a processing analysis of action would involve examining such processes as perception, cognitive decision making, formation of a motor program, execution, and feedback. Such test batteries as the one devised by Laszlo and Bairstow (1985) is a good example of this approach.

Tests can thus be categorized according to a number of different criteria, and almost certainly these will relate directly to the aims of the test. The following is a selection of assessment instruments that have been popular with different professionals when diagnosing children with disorders of coordination. It is not a comprehensive survey of tests. Each test described represents a different type of test; for example, the Touwen is typical of a neurodevelopmental test; the Kinesthetic Sensitivity Test represents those instruments where the underlying cause of the disorder is being addressed; the Bruininks is a popular functional test, whereas the Ayres looks at both underlying process and cause in addressing motor and other disorders. The Griffiths is an example of a general developmental test from which specific motor items can be extracted. Last, the Movement ABC (Henderson & Sugden, 1992) is described in detail to show the authors' own preference and the reasons for this selection.

ASSESSMENT INSTRUMENTS

Southern California Sensory Integration Test
(Ayres, 1972)

Ayres (1972), in her assessment instrument, aims to understand perceptual and motor difficulties in children who have learning or behavior disorders. She designed a battery of 17 items for use with children aged $4\frac{1}{2}$ to 8 years. Children are tested on all 17 items, and the profile of results helps to differentiate four types of sensory integrative dysfunctions underlying a disorder. A combination of scoring procedures produces raw scores that are converted to standard scores by reference to tables. From the results of factor analysis, four clusters of scores are obtained; 7 of the items make up form and space perception, 11 of the items make up praxis, 6 make up postural and bilateral integration, and 3 make up tactile defensiveness. Dysfunction is diagnosed by poor performance in one or more of the clusters.

Laszlo and Bairstow (1985) list four critical observations of the assessment instrument. They first question the validity of many of the test items when placed against the aim of measuring disorders of sensory integration. Second, they argue that there is no clear rationale for the four groups of sensory integrative disorder categories. However, they do agree that some of the groupings appear reasonable, particularly the ones making up the praxis subgroup. Their third criticism involves the tenuous link between the four sensory integrative disorders and different types of learning disorders, particularly when both of these concepts are not adequately defined by Ayres. Last, they note that the diagnosis leads to remediation of the integrative disorder and the neural disorder that underpins it, a view that has been strongly criticized (Cratty, 1981). Laszlo and Bairstow (1985) do finish with some heartening words for Ayres' test and work. They note that she has been the champion for the role of sensory information in normal and abnormal behavior, a role that could have been lost or diminished in influence without her work.

Bruininks-Oseretsky Test of Motor Proficiency (Bruininks, 1978)

This test is a comprehensive instrument based on the original Oseretsky Tests (Oseretsky as cited in Lassner, 1948) and assesses the motor functioning of children from $4\frac{1}{2}$ to $14\frac{1}{2}$ years of age by the use of 46 test items. These items are grouped into eight subtests of running speed and agility, balance, bilateral coordination, strength, upper limb coordination, response speed, visual motor control, and upper limb speed and dexterity. Both a fine and gross motor composite score can be obtained in addition to a general score. A complex scoring system involves test results being weighted and rescaled. The test is intended for use by clinicians, educators, and researchers to enable them to evaluate motor dysfunctions and provide information from which to develop intervention programs. The authors give guidelines for interpreting the results of the test, recommending that certain minimum levels of discrepancy between various subtest and composite scores are required before a difference is considered to be significant.

Laszlo and Bairstow (1985) offer a number of critical comments on the test. First, they criticize the item selection as not being in line with the authors' own criteria for selection. For example, contrary to the authors' stated intention, it is quite easy to fail an item due to perceptual rather than motor deficiencies. They also question whether, because of the high number of pass-fail items, the test can finely discriminate in the manner it purports. Their second critical observation relates to the calculation of composite scores. They point to rather idiosyncratic and the often arbitrary manner in which this occasionally has taken place. Last, when the subtests are totaled, validity questions are raised about response speed and upper limb speed and dexterity contributing equally to the Gross Motor Composite score when the former contains 1 item and the latter, 8 items. Laszlo and Bairstow do note some of the advantages of the Bruininks Test. For the assessment of normal motor development, the same items are used throughout the test, making easy comparisons between ages, and norms are available both for subtests and composite and overall scores. However, they heavily criticize the use of composite scores without allowing for the analysis of individual items. In addition, they quote examples of the subtests themselves showing that they are not independent of each other. Laszlo and Bairstow conclude by stating that the test is most suitable for assessing the overall gross and fine motor abilities of children with mild to moderate nonspecific motor difficulties, but it is not good for differential diagnosis of developmental problems nor for diagnosing underlying causes of a specific confirmed motor disorder.

The Abilities of Young Children Test
(Griffiths, 1970)

A number of tests are available that measure coordination as part of a larger assessment of a child's functioning. An example of this is Griffiths's The Abilities of Young Children Test. The test covers six scales of assessment that cover the whole range of abilities in children from birth to 8 years of age. These scales include a locomotor scale, speech scale, hearing and speech scale, hand-eye coordination scale, a scale of performance tests, and practical reasoning. In years 1 and 2, each scale contains 24 items, whereas in years 3 to 8, only 6 items are included. Three of the scales involve the assessment of motor abilities—locomotor, hand-eye coordination, and performance. In all scales, each item is scored in a pass-fail manner, and the child is credited with a half a month for each item passed in years 1 and 2, and 2 months for each one passed in years 3 to 6. Testing begins below the child's chronological age, so if a child of 5 begins on the age 4 scale and passes all of the items, then passes all of the items on the age 5 scale and three of the items on the age 6, the child would be credited with a test age of 6 years, 6 months.

Laszlo and Bairstow (1985) offer four of what they describe as critical observations of the Griffiths method of assessment. They agree that the scales are relatively well-equated for difficulty, but there are questions concerning the independence of each scale. Second, there is a lack of continuity of items within scales between years. A child being assessed at age 3 will have a different type of item in ages 4 through 8. Thus the concept of abilities is one that is difficult to hold. Third, there is a lack of uniformity in the design of the scale across ages, with more items for younger children, thus being contrary to the principle of development that behavior becomes more diverse and complex with increasing age. The scoring is also different at different ages, with a child of 3 and above having to fail all six items at an age level for testing to be terminated, whereas for ages 1 and 2, only one quarter of the items have to be failed for the testing to finish. Last, testing can be done on children older than the standardized ages of birth to 8, with the assumption that an older physically disabled youngster who scores the same as a younger child has the same so-called mental age. Laszlo and Bairstow do not recommend it for someone wishing to specifically measure motor development, but say it may be useful as an initial assessment for a child with multiple needs. We have chosen to describe the Griffiths because it is a typical example of an assessment instrument widely used with young children, which picks up motor abilities as one part of the child's overall functioning. Although these types of test are useful in infancy, they are too "coarse-grained" for a detailed examination of motor abilities in young children.

Kinesthetic Sensitivity Test
(Laszlo & Bairstow, 1985)

Kinesthesia, sometimes referred to as *proprioception,* is that sense that gathers information from a number of sources to provide knowledge about the body's position and movement, and several authors have noted its contribution to skilled performance and learning (Laszlo & Bairstow, 1985; Schmidt, 1991; Sugden, 1990). Laszlo and Bairstow in a number of articles have examined kinesthesia: how it develops and its relationship to skilled performance in children. From this research work, they developed the Kinesthetic Sensitivity Test (KST), which is designed to give some insights into why a child may have a motor disorder. Along with other researchers,

Laszlo and Bairstow have shown that not only is kinesthesis influential in the control of movement but also that children with known movement difficulties are poorer in their kinesthetic abilities than children whose movements are adequate (Bairstow & Laszlo, 1981; Hulme, Smart, & Moran, 1982; Laszlo & Bairstow, 1980, 1983, 1985).

The influence of kinesthesis on skilled performance is derived from closed-loop theories of motor behavior, which emphasize the perceptual, cognitive, and motor aspects in motor control. A sensory feedback loop provides the system with information about the ongoing movement, particularly, errors enabling corrections to take place through the reprogramming of the movement. It is particularly important when movements are well-practiced, and visual information is no longer required.

The test of Laszlo and Bairstow was designed to be used in research, as a diagnostic tool, and to assist in intervention programs that employed kinesthetic training. The test included two items:

1. Test of kinesthetic acuity: This involved the child having to discriminate the heights of two "runways" through the hands without the use of vision.

2. Test of kinesthetic perception and memory of movement patterns: Here, the child traces a pattern in a template that can be rotated. A masking box is used so the child cannot see the template and can only use kinesthetic information. The masking is then removed and the template rotated to a different position, and the child is asked to reorientate the pattern back to the position it was when he or she was tracing it.

Developmental norms have been provided by Laszlo and Bairstow (1980, 1983, 1985), and the natural progression from this was to extend the test into an examination of children with difficulties and last, for the approach to provide guidelines for intervention. Later in the book, we describe and evaluate some of the intervention work using this type of approach. If one examines the validity of the KST, there are logical arguments to make in its favor. First, it is well-established that kinesthesis plays an important role in the performance and learning of motor skills, and thus, to target such an area would appear to be appropriate. Second, Laszlo and Bairstow have shown that kinesthetic ability does develop during childhood. Third, they have been able to demonstrate that some children with movement difficulties do differ from their normal counterparts on the task. Fourth, by targeting the area of kinesthesis in remediation programs, they have been able to demonstrate improvement in overall motor behavior. Last, it is sensible to look at underlying processes in any difficulties because addressing these rather than surface behaviors will facilitate transfer and generalization to a number of specific skills in the same domain.

There are also criticisms of the test that do cause concern, however. At a theoretical level, the Test covers two parts of kinesthesis—acuity and inter-modal memory—whereas kinesthesis is multifaceted, with the total picture being made up of limb position, starting and finishing of a movement, speed, and acceleration. The total kinesthetic picture emerges from multiple inputs that are then used dynamically for the basis of action. There are questions as to whether passively guided movements as used in the KST can provide this total input. In addition, the scoring procedure has been claimed to provide unreliable results (Doyle, Elliott, & Connolly, 1986). A serious concern was raised by Sugden and Wann (1987) who found little relationship between the KST and a normative-based test of motor impairment (Stott et al., 1984) in children with moderate learning difficulties. Further queries about the test were asked by Elliott, Connolly, and Doyle (1988), and a comprehensive evaluation of the remediation effects has recently been completed by Sims, Henderson, Hulme, and Morton (1996a, 1996b) and will be covered in detail in a later chapter.

Examination of the Child with Minor Neurological Dysfunction (Touwen, 1979)

Touwen's examination is an example of an approach looking at neurological deficits underlying a child's motor problems. It is based on a clinical evaluation of the child but only requires rudimentary movements as the clinician attempts to eliminate perceptual and cognitive factors that influence behavior and concentrate on the motor system. The neurological test pro forma involves 11 categories of behavior and through observation, the child is allocated a score. There are no norms, but a clinical decision is made from the profile of the results about the overall integrity of the child's central nervous system. Touwen (1979) uses clusters of neurological signs to diagnose a number of categories. These categories include (a) hemisyndrome, where the neurological signs form a specific unilateral pattern; (b) involuntary movements; (c) associated movements; (d) developmental retardation; (e) difficulty in coordination, such as clumsiness or awkwardness; (f) sensory disturbances; and (g) neurological profile.

Laszlo and Bairstow (1985) point out that an absence of neurological signs does not confirm brain integrity nor that an aberrant behavior is not present, and conversely, nor do specific signs always indicate a causal relationship with a specific behavioral disorder, simply confirming that the relationship between neurological signs, known brain disorders, and specific behaviors is variable. Laszlo and Bairstow also criticize the absence of any norms and the assessment based on variable observation, and they also note the limited range of tests of voluntary motor behavior.

Test of Gross Motor Development
(Ulrich, 1985)

This Test of Gross Motor Development (TGMD) covers the age range from 3 to 10 years and is intended to be used by teachers of young children. It is a standardized criterion-referenced instrument that is also process-oriented and involves 12 gross motor skills that have been subdivided into locomotor (run, skip, jump, etc.) and object control (catch, strike, throw, etc.). The test is scored on a pass-fail basis for each of three or four performance criteria, and their sums produce a raw score for each subtest.

The content validity of the TGMD was established by three content experts agreeing that the content did represent the major area specified. Construct validity was first established by the use of factor analysis with all 12 items loading on a single dimension; second, there was a high correlation between the results and chronological age, and last, the three experts stated that the descriptive criteria were usable and accurate. Langendorfer (1986) criticized the fact that the criteria are referenced to mature performance rather than using intermediate or even primitive templates for comparison. The scoring system also only gives a single criterion level, further leading the tester to believe there is only one way of doing things, and that is the mature performance. The reliability of the test is quite acceptable with correlation coefficients around the 0.8 mark for the internal consistency of the test, and only a small percentage of the total variance was accounted for by inter-observer or test-retest variability.

A normative sample of 900 children was used, which was stratified for gender, race, community size, and geographical area. In the test construction, Ulrich employed item analysis to arrive at his final 12 items, and norms were set for boys and girls together because of the lack of gender differences. This is something that goes against most of the current literature. The test is easy to administer, with a comprehensive and easy to follow manual.

Overall, the test is well-constructed, has good validity and reliability checks, and it can be used in a norm-referenced or criterion-referenced manner. Langendorfer (1986) in his review believes that although it is more of a motor control test rather than a true development test, it does represent a substantial step forward in assessing young children's gross motor performance. However, it does leave out a large part of the motor domain, namely, fine motor skills.

Movement Assessment Battery for Children (Henderson & Sugden, 1992)

We have reviewed a number of tests that have been used to measure mild to moderate disorders of movement. One of the authors (Sugden) has been involved in the development of an assessment package that is widely used in Europe, Southeast Asia, and Australia, though not as common in the United States. In many recent studies involving DCD, it has been the instrument most widely used for identification of the children (see special issue of *Adapted Physical Activity,* ["Developmental," 1994]). We are therefore describing this test in more detail as it is becoming the test most widely used, and we are intimately associated with it, knowing well its strengths and weaknesses.

The Movement Assessment Battery for Children (Movement ABC) is an integrated package that has evolved over a period of about 30 years. The assessment component of the Movement ABC has two parts: (a) a performance test to be individually administered and requires the child to perform a series of motor tasks and (b) a checklist that is completed by an adult who is knowledgeable of the child's everyday functioning. The Movement ABC combines quantitative and qualitative assessment in its concern for the identification and description of impairments of motor functions in children. The test and checklist are used in different yet complementary ways; the checklist can be used as a screening instrument and the test as a more detailed diagnostic instrument. Together, they can give a reasonably complete picture of a child's motor functioning by examining performance against normative data (test) and by analyzing the child in different contexts (checklist).

Movement ABC Test

The Movement ABC test is the result of development work starting in 1966, the introduction of the first TOMI (Stott et al., 1972), its revision in 1984, and the Movement ABC in 1992. The original TOMI was based on the Oseretsky test of Motor Proficiency as was the substantial revision in 1984. In this revision, the TOMI was organized into three sections covering Manual Dexterity, Ball Skills, and Balance. Age-related norms were produced for items in these three categories. The rationale for the organization of the test into the three sections of manual dexterity, ball skills, and static and dynamic balance first done in 1984 (TOMI) and retained in the Movement ABC, contains a number of components. First, manual dexterity has a face-valid importance with much of what children learn coming from their manual interaction with the environment. In addition, some form of fine motor ability assessment is present in every developmental test involving a motor component. Second, some form of balance test is required in almost every existing instrument assessing motor functioning, and balance is involved in practically every motor activity in which we participate. Last, the argument for ball skills is so strong from a cultural standpoint that their inclusion was deemed to be necessary.

The test is divided into four age bands with a group of activities for each age band, and a differently colored form and separate norms for each age. The age bands and their corresponding ages are as follows:

Band 1: Ages 4, 5, & 6

Band 2: Ages 7 & 8

Band 3: Ages 9 & 10

Band 4: Ages 11 & 12

Eight items are in the test for each age band, and a raw score is recorded for the child's performance on each item; these raw scores are then converted to scaled scores. Three subscores from the different sections of balance, ball skills, and manual dexterity are summed for an overall score. This total motor impairment score is the most important as it summarizes the scores on the eight items and is then interpreted in the light of the percentile norm tables. The cut-off points that represent the 5th and 15th percentile are the ones considered to be most useful, with children falling below the 5th percentile as having a motor problem and requiring additional help as soon as possible and those between the 5th and 15th percentile considered to be borderline, with a recommendation that ongoing monitoring take place using the Movement ABC checklist.

When the test is being used to plan an intervention program, three types of qualitative information should be used. First, motor observations are recorded as to how the child performs motor tasks, noting such aspects as body positions, associated movements, amount of force, and space required. Second, there are behavioral observations on how the child performs in the testing situation, such as impulsivity or distractibility. There are 12 such descriptors, and the same 12 are found in the fifth section of the Movement ABC checklist. Last, some children may have a physical difficulty, such as a vision problem, that may affect the score, and this should be recorded.

Movement ABC Checklist

The second part of the Movement ABC is the checklist specifically designed to assess functional competence in realistic everyday situations. The basis of the checklist is a theoretical analysis of the movement context as proposed originally by Gentile, Higgins, Miller, & Rosen (1975) and extended by Spaeth-Arnold (1981) and Keogh and Sugden (1985). The starting point for the framework is a recognition that an individual performs a task in a contextual setting. Thus, when a task is being performed, an examination of both the individual and the state of the environment is required. The individual performs movements either with the body stationary or moving (walking, running, skipping, etc.). In addition, some tasks involve limb manipulation: We can be stationary (buttons, zippers, writing, drawing) or moving (walking and reaching for an object). Similarly, the environment can be either stable or unstable. For example, when a child is walking around a room, the chairs and tables are stationary, providing spatial but no temporal demands. On the other hand, walking on a busy pavement or simply standing still and attempting to catch a ball involves a moving environment with both spatial and temporal demands being placed on the individual.

The framework thus involves four sections:

1. Child stationary, environment stable: The child is not moving around and the environment is stable. The child has to control his or her own movements, and this can be done more or less in his or her own time.
2. Child moving, environment stable: Activities in this section involve the child moving around a stable environment. Environmental demands are still low with all temporal constraints coming from the child, and he or she controls the body with or without the use of upper limbs.
3. Child stationary, environment unstable: The child is stationary but has to respond to a moving environment, which poses both spatial and temporal constraints. The child no longer is just controlling his or her own movements but has to react to moving others or objects.
4. Child moving, environment unstable: Now, the child has not only to respond to a moving environment but also has to control his or her own moving body, thus increasing the temporal and spatial components of the task.

In addition to these sections, a fifth section assesses behaviors that are often seen within a movement skill context. These are not indicators of a movement skill; a skillful or unskillful child could score high or low on this section. They are behaviors that are often seen to accompany movement experiences and that professionals have indicated as being potential problems in the classroom, on the playground, or at home. This section includes such behaviors as overestimation of abilities, impulsivity, overenthusiasm, fearfulness, lack of confidence, and poor planning.

The total checklist involving the five sections contains 50 items. The checklist is scored by deciding which category of response best fits the child's movement behavior. An example from Section 1 illustrates how the first four sections are scored:

The child can demonstrate precision-accuracy by cutting, drawing, tracing, or coloring between lines or over a designated pattern.

Good   *OK*   *Almost*   *Not Close*

In all cases, the person completing the checklist is asked to tick the category that best describes the child's movement or behavior. The tick is changed to a score enabling section and total test scores to be obtained. The score, or profile, can be used in a number of different ways. A total score can be examined with respect to norms for that particular age group. If the child is in the bottom 15%, remediative action can be employed. The profile of the child's score can also be used in a diagnostic manner to address specific concerns that the checklist highlights.

The Movement ABC checklist would probably fall into Henderson's (1987) descriptive approach within traditional methods. It assesses the child at a functional level in everyday performance, and composite scores can be obtained.

Independent reviews of the instrument have concentrated on the earlier versions (Stott et al., 1972, 1984) that did not contain the checklist and only included the test. Laszlo and Bairstow (1985) note that the test is not useful for assessing normal motor development and that there are no ways to assess average or above average ability so no way to examine individual differences within an age level. They do note that it is a useful way of measuring motor impairment and can provide information for the design of intervention programs.

The relationship between the two instruments in the Movement ABC, the test and the checklist, has been the source of criticism (Sugden & Sugden, 1991; Wright & Sugden, 1996b). Both papers have reported that some children identified by one instrument were not identified by the other. As the instruments are different and used in different contexts, this is not totally surprising, but it has led Wright and Sugden (1996b) to advocate that to identify children with coordination disorders, a two-step approach is required. Both the test and the checklist are employed, and to be identified, a child must fail both instruments. Thus, the APA (1994) DSM-IV requirements are satisfied: The test addresses that part of the definition that covers significant motor impairment and the checklist covers that part that addresses difficulties of a functional nature in everyday life.

CONCLUSIONS

Currently, there is no gold standard assessment instrument for the identification of children with DCD. There are numerous instruments and methods that are directly related to the practical and theoretical concerns of the test authors. If one was to ask a primary school teacher which children in her class had motor coordination difficulties, she would almost certainly be able to pick out one or two children whom she would have noticed. However, she may have difficulty in determining exactly what the difficulties were and how they could be categorized. In addition, she may be limited to skills required in her own classroom with little knowledge of those outside. These limitations are not restricted to teachers; professionals using short assessment instruments are locked into the nature of the instrument and the aims for which it was developed.

Despite the above limitations, we can provide some specific guidelines for assessment. First, there is no substitute for a detailed knowledge of a child's competencies across different contexts. Movement skills occur in different environmental settings, and assessment should reflect this. The assessment procedure should reflect the resources the child brings to the situation and the interaction of these resources with environmental demands. Second, a norm-referenced test will provide comparisons in the motor domain, which is an area of knowledge often neglected by professionals. This will also provide evidence for part of the APA's (1994) DSM-IV definition dealing with significant motor impairment. Third, functional assessment of everyday skills not only has a face validity to it but also again relates to the APA's (1994) DSM-IV definition of interference with daily living. In addition, functional assessment of the child moving in context articulates with a dynamical systems explanation of motor development with the internal resources of the child interacting with external constraints.

The different assessment instruments we have outlined, although containing some common elements, do vary in their aims, objectives, and content. They reflect the nature of the rationale behind the test, the theoretical standpoint of the test constructor, and the constraints of time and expense.

These reflections will be shown in the overlapping but different samples selected by each test. In the first chapter, we noted that characteristics and nature of the condition are linked to the assessment process, and this is a transactional relationship. As our instruments become more refined and identify children in different contexts, so we pick up more fine-grained characteristics, thus, presenting a more complete picture of the disorder, which in turn starts to influence the process of test construction.

4

NATURE OF THE DISORDER

The knowledge gained over the past 30 years or so has been extensive, but the nature and form of DCD from the literature has not as yet reached the point where a totally clear picture is presented. Individual aspects of the disorder have been researched highlighting distinctive behaviors. Each report, however, can be seen to reveal the author or authors' own perspective and interest (e.g., perceptual explanations for DCD have been put forward by Hulme and Lord, 1986; kinesthetic explanations by Laszlo and Bairstow, 1985; the role of speed and planning by Geuze and Kalverboer 1994; Missiuna, 1994; and Rösblad and von Hofsten, 1994; and others). The portrayal of children with DCD is influenced in much the same way as the reported prevalence of the disorder, with the assessment and testing procedures influencing what is found. Not only can the assessment procedures bias the findings in a certain direction, but the methods chosen to report the findings will also have an effect.

Two procedures have been used to investigate the nature of DCD. The first and most common is to compare and contrast the behaviors of the children with DCD with those of children classified as not experiencing DCD. This method follows a long-established tradition of intergroup analysis, and distinctive aspects of DCD tackled in this way are well-documented and will be expanded on in the discussion to follow. An underlying question when performing intergroup analysis involves the concept of a syndrome; are differences found between DCD and non-DCD children clear, consistent, and reliable enough to constitute a recognizable syndrome? In addition to intergroup analysis, the disorder can be assessed within the group of children with DCD by way of intragroup analysis. The usual underlying question here involves the issue of homogeneity and whether children with DCD form an homogeneous group. This method of assessing the nature of DCD is not reported nearly as frequently as the intergroup analysis.

INTERGROUP CHARACTERISTICS OF DCD

Early Descriptive Studies

Studies that describe differences between children with and without DCD range from general summaries to documentation of specific behaviors attributed to the disorder. The *British Medical Journal* ("Clumsy," 1962) lists many traits of children they refer to as clumsy, from being in trouble at school through bad behavior, to having difficulties with self-help skills and being awkward in their movements. The signs or symptoms of DCD cited in this publication are all made in comparison to children who, in the words of the authors, are not "backward." Walton et al. (1962) also refer to the children in their study as clumsy and remark on the group's "excessive clumsiness of movement, poor topographical orientation, inability to draw, to write easily and to copy" (p. 610). In this study, the children's development is charted, and observations are made about the delays of motor milestones in comparison to normally developing children. Although the children with DCD in this study are compared to non-DCD children, the descriptions are done on an individual level.

Gubbay (1975a) went one step further in his description of clumsy children by assessing the children and their matched controls on a screening test consisting of eight motor skills tasks and on the answers to a questionnaire completed by the children's teachers. He found that the clumsy children differed significantly on nearly all the motor skills tasks and all the topics dealt with by the questionnaire, such as poor handwriting, low sporting ability, poor academic performance, bad conduct, clumsiness, fidgetiness, and unpopularity as compared to their non-DCD peers.

During the 1970s and early 1980s, papers were produced that continued to demonstrate the difficulties that children with DCD had in comparison to their peers. The content of these papers became more sophisticated because the information provided was gained in a scientific manner and was therefore more easily replicated than the previous general summaries of children with DCD. Examples of these studies are the Keogh et al. (1979) paper about kindergarten boys, both DCD and non-DCD, followed over 2 years and assessed using a teacher-rated checklist, classroom observations, and a motor skills test, and the Roussounis et al. (1987) study that describes the poor results on a standardized test of motor performance that children with DCD achieved in relation to their general abilities. The papers took on a generally recognizable form, with standardized tests being used and the inclusion of control subjects to compare the results against.

Testing procedures not only became more sophisticated but also more comprehensive. Henderson and Hall (1982) included in their comparative study of DCD and non-DCD children neurodevelopmental examinations, ratings of the children's drawings, scores on a motor impairment test, and an IQ and reading test to determine the characteristics of so-called clumsy children compared to the matched control subjects. The children were originally classified as having DCD by their teachers, and Henderson and Hall (1982) note that this technique of initial classification had inherent problems due to the teachers' actions in selecting children whose motor impairment was significantly affecting school work. Of significance within this paper was the notion of subgroups existing within the DCD group. Henderson and Hall actually used the term "sub groups" to describe distinct behaviors seen within the DCD group, such as those children whose motor impairment was an isolated problem from their IQ, reading, and number measures. Another group clustered together because their motor impairment was associated with numerous other problems, such as low academic attainment, social immaturity, and negative attitudes toward school. As studies became more scientific and specialized, underlying causes were also investigated.

UNDERLYING DEFICITS

Perceptual Differences

In attempting to tackle the underlying perceptual causes of DCD, two groups of researchers stand out; the work done by Hulme and associates (Hulme, Biggerstaff, Moran, & McKinlay, 1982; Hulme, Smart, Moran, & McKinlay, 1984; Lord & Hulme, 1987a, 1987b, 1988) on perceptual motor difficulties and Laszlo and Bairstow (1985) and Laszlo et al. (1988) who stressed the kinesthetic difficulties children with DCD experience. Rather than describing the child's problems in terms of the outcomes of motor tests, these researchers were interested in the ways sensory information was processed and used by children with DCD.

Hulme and his colleagues (Hulme, Biggerstaff, Moran, & McKinlay, 1982; Hulme, Smart, Moran, & McKinlay, 1984; Lord & Hulme, 1987a, 1987b, 1988) investigated the processing of visual and kinesthetic information in children with DCD. Using a line-matching task, the children were asked to reproduce the same movements using either visual or kinesthetic perception. The children with DCD showed perceptual impairments when compared to their controls. In addition, Hulme and his associates also found that the children's poor performance on the visual tasks correlated with their motor performance more than the kinesthetic or cross-modal tasks. They argued that poor visual perception, particularly of spatial information, may contribute to the movement difficulties seen in children with DCD. In a follow-up study to assess the range of visuospatial perceptual judgments in children with DCD, Lord and Hulme (1987b) presented results that indicated a wide-ranging and serious impairment in perceptual processing in the DCD children. Visual acuity was tested to rule out visual-sensory impairments using eye charts and sensitivity tests. These tests showed that the children with DCD were not hindered in this respect. (Confirmation of poor ophthalmic function not being a contributory factor to DCD was reported by Mon-Williams et al., 1994.) Visuospatial perception was measured, testing shape, area, slope, spatial, and linear length discrimination. In each of these tests, there were significant differences between the control children and those with DCD. Although Lord and Hulme (1987b) accept that poor perceptual judgments cannot account for all the difficulties that children with DCD experience, they feel that this aspect of the disorder should be given more prominence and that treatment should include a perceptual training program in its efforts to help the child with DCD, a stance supported by Murphy and Gilner (1988).

Dwyer and McKenzie (1994) found a visual memory deficit, which impaired the accurate reproduction of geometric patterns that were either seen as a whole or presented sequentially, when reproduction of the seen pattern was delayed by 15 seconds after presentation. Without the 15-second delay, children with DCD were able to recall and reproduce the patterns as accurately as their matched controls, suggesting that the time delay requiring the use of stored memory representations led to a decrement in performance, probably due to a difference in visual rehearsal strategies that distinguishes the children with DCD from their well-coordinated peers (Dwyer & McKenzie, 1994). Skorji and McKenzie (1997) took this notion of differences in rehearsal strategies one step further when they examined the capacity of children with DCD to reproduce short sequences of simple movements immediately after presentation and with a 15-second delay. In the Skorji and McKenzie study, the 15-second delay contained four kinds of interference, namely, visual or kinesthetic interference with either a high or a low spatial component. Their findings for immediate recall matched the results of Dwyer and McKenzie (1994) in that there was no difference found between the DCD and non-DCD children. However, when the interference dimensions were included in the recall tests, it was found that the children with DCD only differed from the control children after visual interference with a high spatial involvement was presented. It is interesting that Skorji and McKenzie (1997) also found that kinesthetic interference with either a high or low spatial component did not impair the recall of the modelled movements for either the experimental or control children. The paper concludes that children with DCD are more dependent on visuospatial rehearsal than control children when attempting to memorize modelled movements.

Kinesthetic Differences

Kinesthetic, or proprioceptive, information offers critically important data from within the body about the position and movement of joints, forces in muscles, and orientation in space that contribute to the control of movements. The perceptual information gained from kinesthesis affects the production of movements as the sensory information is translated from the multiple, complex receptors (such as the vestibular apparatus in the inner ear, the receptors in the joint capsules, the muscle spindles embedded in the muscle belly, the Golgi tendon organs, and the cutaneous receptors for haptic sense) and are processed to offer the performers data to control and adapt their movements (Schmidt, 1991).

Laszlo and colleagues (Laszlo & Bairstow, 1985; Laszlo et al., 1988), like Lord and Hulme, adopted a process-orientated approach to investigate the nature of DCD in respect to diagnosis and to treatment. The basis for their work comes from studies in the early 1980s on kinesthetic development in children (Laszlo & Bairstow, 1983) and their work on the contribution of kinesthesis to motor control. Their work emphasized the poor results seen in children with DCD on tasks that emphasized kinesthetic acuity, perception, memory, and velocity discrimination. After kinesthetic training, the children with DCD were seen to improve their overall motor skill performance so demonstrating the significant role that kinesthetic sensitivity plays in motor control (Laszlo et al., 1988). However, it must be noted that in a study by Lord and Hulme (1987a), the KST (Laszlo & Bairstow, 1985) was unable to differentiate between a clinically defined group of children with DCD and a group of age-matched controls. Sugden and Wann (1987) found that the KST had very low correlations with a general test of motor impairment. In addition, Elliot et al. (1988) claimed that the methods involved in collecting data using the KST yielded unreliable results, and Polatajko et al. (1995) found in her study that children with DCD treated with kinesthetic training were not able to spontaneously apply and generalize their increased kinesthetic acuity into increased motor performance of other skills. Sims et al. (1996a, 1996b) do offer further data on the role of kinesthetic training programs for children with DCD. In their first study, Sims et al. (1996a) found no differential effect between two groups of children, both with DCD, when one group was offered no treatment, whereas the other received kinesthetic training, but on a second study, Sims et al. (1996b) compared three groups, one receiving no intervention, one receiving kinesthetic training, and a third group who received a program designed explicitly to avoid reference to kinesthetic training. Children who received no intervention program failed to improve their performance, whereas both groups receiving help improved significantly, with neither group being better than the other (for details, see Chapter 6).

Feedback and Motor Programming Differences

The theme of investigating and assessing DCD using an information-processing model is seen not only in studies that explore the perceptual or input stage of the model but also in studies concentrating on the role of feedback and motor programming. Lord and Hulme (1988) found that although the patterns of movements between two groups of children on a rotary pursuit tracking task were similar, the children with DCD were poorer performers when time on target was considered. It was concluded that although the children with DCD were not limited by an ability to develop a motor program for the rotary pursuit task, they were restricted by impaired visual feedback control. The reasons cited for this impairment, in contrast to the control subjects, were difficulties with visual detection of errors, selection and execution of corrective responses, appropriate timing of responses, and attentional factors. It is suggested that children with DCD are slow in processing information that affects other aspects of motor control, such as responding to errors, but that they do have a representation of what is needed to be done.

Smyth and Glencross (1986) suggested that children with DCD are deficient in speed of processing kinesthetic information but not in speed of processing visual information. Using chronometric techniques (one or two choice reaction time tasks), their findings suggested that DCD is associated with a dysfunction in proprioceptive information processing but not with an impairment in the response selection process. The children with DCD were no different than the non-DCD children when it came to processing visual information. Care must be taken in accepting the results from the Smyth and Glencross study because the children in the DCD group represented an incidence rate of 20% to 30% being classified as experiencing DCD, a very high rate compared to other studies. The choice of tasks in this study were also relatively easy in comparison to those conducted by Hulme and colleagues (Hulme, Biggerstaff, Moran, & McKinlay,1982; Hulme, Smart,

Moran, & McKinlay, 1984; Lord & Hulme, 1987a, 1987b, 1988) so possibly allowing for fewer differences to emerge in movement preparation seen in the speed of visual reaction time.

Differences in Speed of Decision Making

Finding only small and insignificant differences between children with DCD and their matched controls in their abilities to process visual feedback, van der Meulen, Denier van der Gon, Geilen, Gooskens, & Willemse (1991) supported the findings of Smyth and Glencross (1986). They suggested that the increased time delay the children with DCD showed when trying to track a target was a consequence of a strategy they employed to deal with their difficulties in motor performance and not due merely to impaired information processing. Wann (1987) suggested a similar argument to explain the less mature patterns of movements seen in poor handwriting, where the weak writers employed movements that allowed greater visual control during movement execution. Again, this can be seen as a strategy used to compensate for difficulties in motor performance, with a need to rely more heavily on visual feedback from the writing movements.

Rösblad and von Hofsten (1994) manipulated visual information during a task that required children to pick a bead from a cup and transport it to another cup. Using mirrors and a curtain, visual information about the hand, cups, and beads were manipulated. The results showed that the children with DCD demonstrated slower and more variable movements than the control subjects in the first instance but that the removal of visual information affected both sets of children in similar ways. This suggests that the children with DCD were no more or less reliant on visual feedback to control their movements than the control children. Both groups merely slowed down the movement to maintain their accuracy level, this being particularly evident when the whole action, as opposed to only the hand or the target, was obscured. The initial slower and more variable movements of the children with DCD is not then attributable to visual information but could possibly result from poor forward planning, as seen in children given the title of dyspraxic. If a child finds it difficult to plan ahead or anticipate and prepare for difficulties, then errors have to be dealt with as they occur, which interrupts the smoothness and efficiency of movement. Rösblad and von Hofsten (1994) see this maladaptive strategy as being the result of anticipatory monitoring being replaced with feedback monitoring, which is both slower and more variable. The impaired capacity for anticipatory control is seen as a limiting factor for children with DCD.

These studies seem to agree that children with DCD have slower movements than their matched controls, but each paper offers slightly different explanations for this slowness. The explanations begin with perceptual aspects of the information-processing model being cited as impaired but move onto aspects of processing that link the input of information to the cognitive aspects of information processing, such as strategy development and anticipation. The intertwined role of these two features of information processing, input and decision making, appears to be significant.

Another aspect of information processing is the central decision-making capacity of children with DCD, and this too has been tackled by comparing the performance of control subjects in a laboratory setting by asssssing motor response processing through simple or choice reaction time tasks. The research of van Dellen and Geuze (1988) found that the slowness of children with DCD was largely localized in the cognitive decision process response selection, which they felt could be due to inefficient response organization or poor movement execution. The children with DCD in their study were slower to respond to stimuli but not inaccurate in their movements. In a second study, van Dellen and Geuze (1990) found that children with DCD were slower than their controls in executing simple, fast, goal-directed hand movements only when the movement accuracy demands were relatively high. This finding was substantiated by Vaessen and Kalverboer (1990) in their study, where they found that motor tasks requiring greater accuracy constituted a heavier load for children with DCD than those with time pressures. Missiuna (1994) also reports that children with DCD are detrimentally affected by an increase in the accuracy requirement of a task. This could be because the children with DCD need more time to receive and process feedback or to lock onto the target so extending the target phase of the movement. Possibly, the children with DCD underestimate the requirements of the higher movement accuracy demands and as a result, need more time to adjust their inappropriate movements. This could be due to inaccuracy in the perception of the accuracy demands or inaccuracy in the planning or programming of such movements.

Henderson et al. (1992) found that when targets were small, children with DCD showed significant differences from controls in duration of time in reaching the target. The children with DCD also demonstrated slower reactions to both simple and choice reaction tasks than controls, which is explained by general resource depletion in the control and planning of action. Attentional resources are stretched as the coordination difficulties known to the children interfere with performance. In a dual-task performance, where children with and without DCD were asked to respond to a reaction time task while walking on a balance beam, it was shown that children with DCD did not perform as well as control children in tasks with both cognitive and motor load (Vaessen & Kalveboer, 1990). It was found that it was not the motor loading that caused the decrement in performance—in this case, a narrower balance beam—but rather, the cognitive loading in terms of the increased accuracy demands made by the reaction time task. The children with DCD demonstrated significantly slower reaction times regardless of the width of the balance beam.

The processes of timing and force control have often been proposed as underlying motor control, and they were investigated in DCD children by Lundy-Ekman, Ivry, Keele, and Woollacott (1991). Their study involved three groups: two were identified as DCD, whereas the third was a control group. The two DCD groups involved one with soft neurological signs associated with cerebellar dysfunction and one with soft neurological signs associated with dysfunction of the basal ganglia. A tapping task, a perception timing task, and a force control task were employed with all subjects. On the tapping task, both DCD groups were impaired compared to the control group (with the cerebellar group being particularly variable), suggesting an inability to control the temporal aspects of the movement. On the perception timing task, only the cerebellar DCD group was impaired. On the force control task, the basal ganglia group was more variable than the other two, with the cerebellar group being impaired compared to the control group. The study is important because it shows the difference between two DCD groups and also demonstrates that force and timing are separate components of motor control, and these rely on different neural systems.

The findings of the experiments concerning DCD and information processing suggest that there is evidence of deficits in children with DCD concerning the input side of the information-processing model that are both visual and kinesthetic and that lead to difficulties in error detection and movement correction during execution. These perceptual difficulties result in less efficient motor programming in children with DCD, in particular, when accuracy and anticipation is required. With increases in the complexity and spatial uncertainty of tasks, children with DCD find more and more difficulties with their motor control.

MOVEMENT DIFFERENCES

The nature of DCD has been assessed by investigating the physical differences seen between children with and without DCD, adopting what Larkin and Hoare (1992) term a *movement emphasis* on movement dysfunction. Difficulties in movement are the primary indicators for identifying a child with DCD, yet despite this obvious focal point, research has been mainly directed at the perceptual and sensory processes as the foregoing review has shown. Larkin and Hoare (1992) chose to look at running, jumping, and hopping in children with DCD, making comparisons with well-coordinated children. The children with DCD ran slower than the controls and exhibited decreased stride length and increased stride time along with other factors that contributed to both slower and less efficient running than the controls. Using a standing broad jump, children with DCD were significantly poorer than controls when distance jumped was the measure. It was noted that they produced a reduced movement range with less extension at the knee and hip than controls and were asymmetrical on landing, showing a lack of control not seen in the control children. This reduction in the degrees of freedom used for movements by the children with DCD was seen in their hopping, too. In summary, Larkin and Hoare (1992) found that the patterns of movement seen in the children with DCD were immature and lacking in control in comparison to the control group. These children were unable to time the segmental interactions of their limbs to produce orderly and efficient movements. Some of the children with DCD could coordinate their lower limbs alone, but the linkage between upper and lower limbs was problematic. Overall, the children with DCD were generally slower and were consistently more endomorphic than the controls, and both fitness and size problems would be seen in gross motor skills. Larkin and Hoare (1992) see the size changes in the children with DCD as being important in the cause and effect of movement difficulties.

The lack of motor control reported by Larkin and Hoare (1992) is a topic investigated by Williams and Burke (1995) who assessed children with and without DCD by an examination of their basic patellar reflex response. Williams and Burke hypothesized that there are developmental differences in the input-output properties of the alpha motoneuron pool between children with DCD and controls, which may identify potential nervous system mechanisms underlying motor control difficulties in children with DCD. These differences—in the case of children with DCD, an exaggerated patellar tendon reflex response—may account for their inability to precisely regulate muscle force and their lack of precision in processing proprioceptive feedback. Williams and Burke suggest that the increased sensitivity seen in the patellar tendon reflex (more than twice the amount of force recorded for children with DCD than for controls) reveals that a greater proportion of the alpha motoneuron pool is recruited by the peripheral reflex loop. They propose that the enhanced tendon reflex is due to an increase in muscle spindle gain via the gamma motor system, and they quote supportive works for increases in muscle spindle gain in resting muscle to explain reduced precision in the processing of proprioceptive feedback during movement control. The tentative suggestion is that DCD may be related to central nervous system (CNS) dysfunction and not to a developmental delay, with the CNS being unable to regulate the excitability of the alpha motoneuron pool during the performance of voluntary movements in children with DCD and increased gamma activity affecting spindle mechanisms.

The coordination difficulties experienced by children with DCD may be compounded and reinforced by a desire to avoid physical activity. This withdrawal from physical activities has been seen to reduce the level of fitness and strength of children with DCD when compared to matched controls (O'Beirne et al., 1994). Anaerobic performance and power measures were assessed by O'Beirne et al., and they confirmed the findings of Larkin and Hoare (1992) in respect to the significantly slower running performances of the children with DCD. In addition, they found that there were differences between the children's peak power and power output. Heart rate measures confirmed that the children with DCD were working as hard as their peers during the testing procedures but with less success. The difficulties that the children with DCD showed when producing explosive movements are possibly linked to their poor anaerobic power, which carries over to their low levels of fitness. The children with DCD were also found to be heavier than the controls, possibly another consequence of the movement difficulties that they face, leading to avoidance of exercise and a more sedentary lifestyle.

ADDITIONAL ASSOCIATED BEHAVIORAL DIFFERENCES

Apart from the movement difficulties seen in children with DCD, there is evidence that in comparison to non-DCD children, the disorder is accompanied by social and emotional difficulties, such as behavior problems (Losse et al., 1991), low self-esteem (Shaw et al., 1982), poor goal setting, low self-concept with a reduced inclination to accept responsibility (Henderson et al., 1989), isolation, lack of self-confidence, being teased (Kalverboer, DeVries, & van Dellen, 1990), and poor social competence (Kalverboer et al., 1990; Knight, Henderson, Losse, & Jongmans, 1990). The long-term prognosis for these children is not good in general, although some children do catch up with their peers (Cantell et al., 1994; Geuze & Börger, 1993; Losse et al., 1991; Lyytinen & Ahonen, 1989). Kalverboer et al. (1990) found that children who their teachers rated as clumsy were also often considered as withdrawn, submissive, and self-conscious. Gubbay (1975a) felt that the perceived awkwardness of children with DCD, as seen in their play and sporting behaviors, led to rejection by their classmates. This isolation of children with DCD is also reported by Kalverboer et al. (1990). In their study, they felt that the children with DCD lacked self-confidence, possibly through a reaction to the difficulties they experienced with socially important skills. This in turn prevented their involvement in play and sports. The children further isolated themselves to avoid overt rejection. In the same study, it was found that children with DCD attempted to cover up their difficulties by exhibiting disruptive behaviors in class, a point noted by Keogh et al. (1979).

Emotional and Behavioral Difficulties

More recently, Losse et al. (1991) reported that children with DCD were often bullied, had poor concentration, and were more disorganized in class than their well-coordinated peers. In essence, Losse et al. found that the children with DCD had more behavioral problems than their matched controls. Henderson et al. (1989) showed that children with movement difficulties were unrealistic in the way they set goals for themselves, had lower self-esteem, and were less inclined to accept responsibility for what might happen to themselves. The children in this study were seen to frequently set goals for themselves without regard for the feedback given to them, and the children then set themselves unrealistically high goals. A possible explanation for this is that if one sets an impossibly high standard of achievement, then success is unlikely, and the impact of failing is reduced. A further extension of this is children with DCD being less likely to accept responsibility for their own behavior, and Henderson et al. note that if events are not in your control, then one can afford to set unrealistic goals.

Inherent in the research on the associated difficulties in children with DCD is that the school environment exacerbates or contributes in some way to these behaviors. The fact that importance is attached to proficiency in physical activities places the child with DCD in a stressful situation. Wright and Sugden (1997) found a significant difference between children with DCD and their well-coordinated peers when behavioral problems related to motor difficulties performed during the school day were identified by the children's schoolteachers.

Although much of the research that has taken place in this area studied children with DCD who were 8 years old or older, Schoemaker and Kalverboer (1994) were interested to see if children with DCD had various social and affective difficulties earlier in life. They found that even by the age of 6 or 7 years, children with DCD had fewer playmates and were asked to play less often than their peers. Both parents and teachers of the children with DCD judged them to be more introverted, more serious, more insecure, more isolated, and less happy than their matched controls. The children also reported that they were aware of their difficulties. Whatever the degree of DCD, the children experienced these social and personal difficulties.

COMMENTS ON THE
INTERGROUP DESIGN

Support for the experimental design of using matched controls to highlight the differences between two groups of children comes from Henderson et al. (1992). Provided care is exercised in the matching procedure, they believe that detailed, pertinent information can be gleaned about impaired processes from research using a design that incorporates matched controls. Many aspects of developmental coordination disorder have been discovered, confirmed, and highlighted using this technique, as the review has shown. Each separate study advances the knowledge and understanding of what underlies DCD, but whether it will ever be possible to produce a cohesive theoretical account from such divergent sources remains unclear (Henderson, 1992).

One negative aspect of this method of investigating DCD is the inherent presumption that the children with DCD all demonstrate the behaviors in question. However, in spite of the many different methods that have been used to identify children with DCD, ranging from referrals by the medical profession and concern from parents to the array of skills tests conducted by different researchers in different countries, there is a stability about their findings. Experimental designs, including control children that have made group-based findings on a variety of characteristics of children with DCD, do appear to concur. In some papers, the particular experiment conducted to establish the occurrence of a certain behavior in children with DCD may include the notion that not all the children exhibit this behavior to the same extent. We suggest that the nature of DCD is such that the impairments seen in some children are not evident in others. In other words, DCD means different things to different children, and although there may be children who share similar difficulties, there are also children who are different. The next section of this chapter will attempt to show that children with DCD differ sufficiently from within their own groupings to warrant intragroup analysis of the disorder.

INTRAGROUP CHARACTERISTICS OF DCD

The second and much less common approach to examining the nature of DCD is to investigate the differences exhibited within the DCD group. Researchers have often commented that children with DCD form a heterogeneous group, in that the movement patterns that they display are different in different children (Cantell et al., 1994; Dare & Gordon, 1970; Dewey & Kaplan, 1994; Gubbay, 1975a; Henderson, 1992; Henderson & Hall, 1982; Hoare, 1994; Larkin & Hoare, 1992; Sugden, 1972; Sugden & Sugden, 1991; Wright & Sugden, 1996a, 1996c).

The Severity of DCD

The extent to which the children experience movement difficulties is the factor that is most commonly used to discriminate one subgroup of children from another. Sugden and Sugden (1991) use the notion of children *at risk* and children with *movement problems* when referring to the severity of the disorder. The cut-off points in norm-referenced tests, such as the TOMI (Stott et al., 1984) and the Movement ABC (Henderson & Sugden, 1992), offer indications of severity by reference to percentile charts. It is possible, however, to place children with DCD in subgroups from within the group on the basis of severity and on the nature of the disorder.

Sugden (1972) subdivided children with DCD both by the severity of the disorder and motor and behavioral traits that grouped the children together. For example, he grouped a set of boys who not only had the greatest movement difficulties but who were also seen to evidence the characteristics of hesitancy and forgetfulness in the starting and execution of a movement. The subdivisions were made on the basis of information from a teacher-rated checklist. The drawing ability of children with DCD was investigated by Barnett and Henderson (1992), where the children were compared to control subjects but with the addition of observations made about differences within the DCD group. Again, severity was a distinguishable factor mentioned in this study, linked to a note that there appeared to be a group of children whose difficulties prevailed over time, particularly in older children. This distinguishing feature of continued difficulties for some but not all children with DCD is reported in other studies, too (Cantell et al., 1994; Losse et al., 1991).

Barnett and Henderson (1992) also report that, whereas the children with DCD in their drawing study had poor scores on motor control and coordination, they differed on three other measures: representation of proportions, depiction of particular features, and awareness of detail in any feature.

Subgrouping by Motor Performance

The most comprehensive reports detailing subgroups of children with DCD are those by Hoare (1991, 1994), Dewy and Kaplan (1994), and Wright and Sugden (1996a). Hoare (1994) has reported on subgroups of children with DCD by examining the results of the children's performance on kinesthetic, visual, cross-modal (kinesthetic and visual), and fine and gross motor tasks, amounting to a battery of 32 perceptual and motor tasks. Subtypes of DCD were established using statistical approaches, such as factor analysis. Five patterns of movement dysfunction emerged from the factor analysis, and Hoare (1991) named them *manual dexterity, gross body coordination, vision, balance/hop,* and *active kinesthesis.* Following the factor analysis with cluster analysis, five subgroups of children with DCD were isolated. One group found motor tasks difficult in the absence of perceptual problems. Another group had difficulties across both motor and perceptual domains. A third group scored well on visual tasks but poorly on tasks requiring kinesthetic processing. In another group, there was dissociation between perceptual tasks, no difficulty with kinesthetic tasks, but less competence on visually loaded tasks in comparison to the rest of the children with DCD. Last, the fifth group had a mixed profile, suggesting some separation of inability within the gross motor domain.

Hoare's (1991, 1994) results demonstrate that although the children with DCD all experienced difficulties with their movements, enough to place them in a generalized group with the title DCD being accredited to them, there were examples of where specific difficulties were far more evident within one subgroup than another. Hoare (1994) does not claim to have discovered consistent subgrouping of the disorder, but she does demonstrate the heterogeneity of the children with DCD that has been suspected and commented on by other researchers and recommends that subgrouping can be an effective end to intervention.

Dewey and Kaplan (1994) examined 51 boys and girls with motor problems between the ages of 6 and 10 years and matched them with a control group showing no motor difficulties. In the motor problem group, there were 44 boys and 7 girls. All were tested on a battery of motor, gesture, and sequencing tests together with language, academic, and perceptual assessments. All children were included in cluster analysis that resulted in four definitive subgroups. These included one with deficits in balance, coordination, and gestural performance; one with deficits in motor sequencing; one with severe deficits across all areas, and one with no difficulties compared with the others. Most of the control group (49 out of 51) were in this final group. This group also contained 12 children from the motor problem group, suggesting that either they were wrongly diagnosed or that their difficulties were minimal. Of particular interest in this study is the separation of the first two groups: one showing difficulties associated with the execution of the motor action with planning remaining intact and one associated with planning processes. This type of typology strongly links to the theoretical underpinnings of the Movement ABC, both in assessment and intervention (Henderson & Sugden, 1992).

The design of the Wright and Sugden (1996a) study, combined with the structure of the two assessment tools contained in the Movement ABC, made it possible to examine the nature of DCD in children from both perspectives: intergroup and intragroup analysis. The children with DCD are compared to their matched peers, who acted as controls, and the nature of their movement difficulties are also assessed from within the group. The within-DCD-group comparison is made possible by the design of the Movement ABC checklist and the Movement ABC test, as the two modes of assessment offer 12 variables from which to analyze the data. The subjects in the Wright and Sugden study were 69 children identified as having a movement problem or at risk according to the Movement ABC.

Both assessment modes from the Movement ABC, namely the checklist and the test results, are used in the study and provided data on 12 variables that were subjected to cluster and factor analysis.

From the factor analysis in the Wright and Sugden (1996a) study, five factors emerged from the data. The factor that accounted for most of the variance within the DCD group was the *fast hands* factor, followed closely by the *catching* factor. The grouping of the variables through the factor analysis was a revealing process in that it highlighted the areas in which the Wright and Sugden sample of children with DCD have particular difficulty. The factor analysis showed that the sections in the Movement ABC checklist where the children are on the move or the environment is changing were clearly grouped together and that the section that deals with stable tasks in a stable environment was a separate issue. The second most robust factor was *catching,* which the multiple-regression model, from a previous study by Wright (1996), predicted would be an important indicator of DCD. This grouping and factor loading supports the findings of Henderson et al. (1992), Missiuna (1994), and Vaessen and Kalverboer (1990).

To test the a priori prediction that the children with DCD would not form a homogeneous group, the standardized scores of the five factors were used as raw data for the cluster analysis. Taking the differing characteristics of these clusters as a starting point for an intervention program would lead to a markedly different model than one proposed from collective data where the children with DCD are considered to be a single, homogeneous group.

The children in the Wright and Sugden (1996a) study from Cluster 1 demonstrate the most even profile of all the clusters, with no large deviations from the mean score. When compared to their peers within the DCD group, this group represented the least impaired of the DCD children. Their results suggested that they need help in all areas but that their difficulties are not as yet severe; possibly, they represent the at-risk children. Hoare (1994) found no similar cluster in her sample of children with DCD, but as every child in her study had multiple criteria for selection into the DCD group, it could be that she included the more severely affected children only, whereas the Wright and Sugden (1996a) study included children from the bottom 15% of a randomly selected population.

The second cluster of children had scored poorly specifically on the factor indicating that particular help was needed to perform throwing, aiming, and receiving. Hoare (1994) had one cluster of children with a specific difficulty that in her case, was the variable visual perception. She suggested that the children in this cluster may have only a visual contribution to their movement dysfunction rather than a generalized perceptual dysfunction. The specific inability of this cluster to master catching objects may be demonstrating a dysfunction separate from other manipulative and functional tasks requiring visual integration.

The third cluster needed most assistance when the environment was changing, but they also exhibited difficulties in the *control of self* factor. Changes in the environment are not under the control of the individual and therefore, need to be dealt with through adaptive behaviors. Anticipation is a factor that can help in dealing with unpredictable situations, and it has been shown that children with DCD are poor at anticipating (Lord & Hulme, 1988). Rösblad and von Hofsten (1994) believe that when children are poor at planning ahead or at anticipating, they slow their movements. This strategy may be of benefit when the child is in control of his or her own timing, but many situations demand a fast response, or failure ensues. These two factors include all the sections from the Movement ABC checklist and so suggest an overall impairment, but in this case, more severe than that seen in the Cluster 1 children. Hoare (1994) found a cluster comprising 15 children out of 80 possible subjects, who demonstrated a profile of difficulties in all but running, compared to the rest of the children with DCD. From her results, she suggested that this cluster had a generalized perceptual dysfunction, so supporting the work of Hulme and Laszlo and colleagues (Hulme, Biggerstaff, Moran, & McKinlay,1982; Hulme, Smart, Moran, & McKinley, 1984; Laszlo & Bairstow, 1985; Laszlo et al., 1988; Lord & Hulme, 1987a, 1987b, 1988). This third cluster also had difficulties in all areas, but their best score was *dynamic balance,* which running certainly demands. These two clusters of children, parted by the South China Sea with one sample from Singapore and the other from Australia, do appear to have difficulties in common.

The children in the fourth cluster demonstrated the most obvious difficulty in one factor of all the clusters. They easily record the highest score on the *fast hands* factor, and added to that, they have the highest score for *dynamic balance.* This cluster of children seems to be the group that requires help most urgently because of their problems in writing, drawing, and other manual skills required in the classroom. In Hoare's (1994) work, she isolated a group of children who showed great difficulty with the Purdue Pegboard (similar to the *fast hands* tasks) and with their static and dynamic balance. This fourth cluster of children, although not showing obvious difficulties with static balance, do demonstrate both manual dexterity and dynamic balance difficulties—far more in fact, than any of the other children with DCD, very similar to Hoare's (1994) findings.

The cluster analysis used by Hoare (1994) to group the children with DCD found clusters of children with DCD who, although being equally impaired overall, were seen to have deficits that generalized across modalities and deficits that were also highly specific. All the children in the Wright and Sugden (1996a) study failed either or both the Movement ABC checklist or test, so placing them in the DCD category, but the factor and cluster analysis has shown that although they may be equally impaired according to test scores, they do not all demonstrate their impairments in the same problematic motor behaviors. Some of the Wright and Sugden children with DCD need urgent help with their manipulative skills, as Cluster 4 has shown, whereas others have their greatest difficulties when involved with ball skills.

Not included for factor and cluster analysis in any of the three studies are the associated behaviors related to motor difficulties, dealt with in Section 5 of the Movement ABC checklist. These behaviors may give cause to further subtypes if the purpose of this exercise is to plan a management program for children with DCD. Examining the data from the Wright and Sugden (1996a) clusters reveals some patterns of associated behaviors reported by the teachers through the results of Section 5 in the Movement ABC checklist. Those in Cluster 3, considered to be a group of children with many difficulties, show the clearest pattern of associated behaviors related to their motor difficulties.

In particular, they are seen to be easily distracted, lacking in persistence, disorganized, and confused about their school tasks. This group of children scored poorly on the *changing environment* factor, the worst of all the children with DCD. The reported associated behaviors for this cluster would interact to make adjustments to a changing environment difficult for a child with coordination difficulties. Cluster 4 also shows a profile of being easily distracted, looking around and responding to noises and movements outside of the classroom environment. This may add to the causes of the poor scores this group of children had on manual dexterity tasks done under a time constraint. The information given in Section 5 of the Movement ABC checklist offers pertinent information when addressing the issue of the nature of DCD.

Sampling procedures do have a significant effect on any subsequent findings. The children included in Hoare's (1994) study were taken from 80 children already identified as having DCD by teachers, doctors, psychologists, or parents and who were referred to a movement education program conducted at an Australian university. Thus, the samples are not entirely comparable. It is likely that the children with DCD in Hoare's study were more noticeably affected by their difficulties than the Wright and Sugden (1996a) cohort, which included the bottom 15% of a random sample. Nevertheless, there are difficulties seen in the clusters from the Singaporean children that are evident in the Australian children, too. The largest group of children with DCD from the Wright and Sugden study are those who appear to have a relatively consistent pattern of difficulties across the board but at a borderline level. This possible at-risk group of children is not seen in Hoare's (1994) study, possibly because of the sample selection procedures. It is interesting to note that the similarities between the clusters in the two studies are found in the clusters other than the large at-risk cluster from Singapore. It could be that having removed the at-risk children from the Singaporean sample, those remaining children were more like the Australian children in Hoare's sample. It is these remaining three clusters where the children appear to have shared difficulties: one cluster from Singapore, who needed most help with their aiming, throwing, and catching skills but otherwise had all their scores above the mean, were similar to an Australian cluster of children who had all but one score above the mean and most difficulty with visual perception. The patterns of difficulties seen in the other two smaller clusters are not dissimilar, either. The Dewey and Kaplan (1994) study was different to the Hoare (1994) and Wright and Sugden (1996a) work in that non-DCD children were included in the analysis. This resulted in one of the four clusters being almost totally composed of the non-DCD children, leaving three factors, which appear to overlap some of the Hoare (1994) and Wright and Sugden (1996a) clusters. An important finding from the Dewey and Kaplan (1994) work is the separation of planning and execution, which if confirmed by subsequent work, will have important intervention implications.

CONCLUSIONS

Intergroup analysis highlights the differences en masse between the children with and without DCD. Many of the tasks children with DCD have difficulty with have been confirmed in samples across the world. These tasks have included functional ones, such as locomotor skills and others involving fine motor demands. In addition, the underlying processes in children with DCD have also been shown to be different to non-DCD controls. These have included differences in the way information is received and processed, such as in the visual and kinesthetic areas through those involving timing and force variables to the processes of motor programming and feedback. In addition, differences in emotional and personal variables, such as self-concept and behavior, have also been found. Whenever a group of movements or tasks are highlighted in the intergroup analysis of the children with DCD to matched controls, the results can be corroborated and reinforced with findings from studies conducted elsewhere, with children from different cultures and in different countries. In all of the individual studies we have analyzed, differences emerge between children with DCD and matched controls. However, no metaanalysis has been performed that pulls together these disparate studies enabling a firm syndrome to be determined. In addition, not enough work on intragroup analysis has been conducted for it to be said that there might be stable subtypes of children with DCD. The three studies reported do require replication if it is felt desirable for subgroups to be identified. There is another line of thought that it is not necessary to do this but simply to identify the child as having difficulties, identify those difficulties, and design a program of intervention accordingly, without the need for specific stable subtypes to be identified. The most striking deposition in the intragroup analysis found from the three studies is that these children do have different profiles, and this may be of use in designing intervention strategies. Relying on results generated from studies that compare children with DCD to their matched controls does not allow for the significant differences found within the children.

5

DEVELOPMENT AND PROGRESSION

ISSUES AND CONCEPTS

In Chapter 2, we examined motor development by describing some of the changes that take place from birth through adolescence and by suggesting explanations for these changes. Principles and concepts derived from normal and pathological development provide us with the fundamental information from which to examine the development and progression of individual conditions, such as coordination disorders. Rutter (1989) outlines a number of these principles, noting that the timing and nature of experiences are complex interactions of biological, psychological, and social processes. There is an expectation that both continuities and discontinuities will occur, with change being a natural part of development, yet because most of our later functioning is based on earlier learning, there will be consistencies. Some continuities include behaviors that may change in form but still reflect the same basic process, a point of considerable importance when examining motor functions from birth through adolescence, with the accompanying increasingly large repertoire of movements in the older individual representing change yet similar underlying difficulties representing consistency.

Possible mediating factors for continuities and discontinuities include genetics in a condition such as autism. Others may have a weaker genetic component, but genes may influence the continuation of the disorder into adult life. Other biological substrates may not be genetically determined but could include pregnancy and birth complications that may have a constitutional effect, such as a neurological disorder emerging in a number of different functional ways. Environmental influences, such as rearing practices, and educational factors are again going to be major influences as the child moves into more demanding and complex contexts.

Rutter (1989) notes that even in some genetic conditions, the transitions and continuities in life are not universal, and huge changes can be brought about at an individual level by some large event or influence. He is suggesting that the influences are so complex that it would be wrong to polarize nature and nurture into mutually exclusive explanations, and the transactions between the various contributing partners appear to be the most comfortable way of explaining continuities and change in children's development.

Issues

Basic questions concerning the origins and progressions of motor disorders in children can be split into a number of smaller and tighter lines of investigation. An obvious question surrounds general etiological issues. In a number of conditions, such as cerebral palsy, there are clear links with variables such as birth weight and gestational age, with more tenuous links with factors such as social and biological qualities of the parents (Stanley, 1984; Stanley & Alberman, 1984). The issue is not as simple as asking what the origins of the condition are but more, what the issues are surrounding the risk of a particular condition. As we move from a known biological disorder, such as cerebral palsy, and move to general motor disorders in children where the biological foundations are not as secure, the link between various antecedent conditions and the disorder is more tenuous. This complexity increases as the child develops.

When examining origins and development, there are a number of age-related issues. For example, if we have a cohort of children with low birth weight (1500 g) and a short gestational age, there will be a higher incidence of children with cerebral palsy (Stanley & Alberman, 1984). However, the question arises about the remainder of the cohort who do not develop cerebral palsy. If we examine those children at entry into school, around 5 years of age, do we find a higher incidence of general motor disorders? Similarly, an investigator can begin by identifying and assessing children for motor difficulties at 5 or 6 years of age and follow them forward longitudinally to monitor their development over the next few years. Are the same children identified at, say, 12 or 16 as those who were identified at 5 or 6? For those who remained the same, were there any experiences that they missed during childhood that may have contributed to any lack of improvement? Of equal importance is to examine children who were having problems at one age and yet these problems seemingly disappeared a few years later.

The phrase, "grow out of it" has been used to describe this phenomenon and could induce complacency in those associated with the child. However, there are two reasons why this complacency is misplaced. First, we will be presenting evidence to show that even if the child shows an improvement in motor behavior, there are often other developmentally associated behaviors, such as poor behavior in school and low academic achievement, which can emerge. The second point is ethical rather than scientific: We are firm believers that if at any time the disorder is providing stress, worry, or anxiety to the child, parent, or other significant person, then it ought to be addressed and some form of intervention put in place.

There are two bodies of literature that deal with the aforementioned questions, although there is some overlap between the two. The first is often medically based and concerns antecedents in the early years, such as birth factors, the status of the infant in those early weeks, and development in the early years up to and including school entry. A second body of literature includes medical literature but also involves studies by psychologists and educators and examines the relationship between early school age motor disorders and the progression during the school years into adolescence.

Concepts

When examining disorders of any kind in children, it is useful to distinguish between the conceptions of the disorders. Capute, Shapiro, and Palmer (1981) proposed a way of assessing motor problems by using the terms *delay, deviance,* and *dissociation:* delay is the lower end of a normal continuum; dissociation is a difference in the rate of development among different abilities, and deviancy indicates that overall development is different rather than simply delayed. Other writers, notably Bishop and Edmondson (1987), although not addressing motor development, have distinguished between the concepts of delay and disorder when analyzing language. The former relates to the extreme tail of a normal distribution of language milestones—or in our case, motor milestones—whereas disorder involves some specific factor that has interfering effects on development, producing more permanent deficits. Bishop and Edmundson produced theoretical models for language development and language-impaired children, and we have reproduced them using motor development and disorder as the dependent variable instead of language (see Figure 5.1).

In Model A in Figure 5.1, children have a slow start and then their motor development progresses at the same rate as normal. The timing of each motor milestone is delayed, but the difference between one milestone and the next is normal, and the children would be described as having a developmental lag in the motor domain. In Models B and C, the problem is more severe, with a slow rate of development in B from the same start, and an early plateau in C possibly suggesting an underlying neurological impairment. In the same

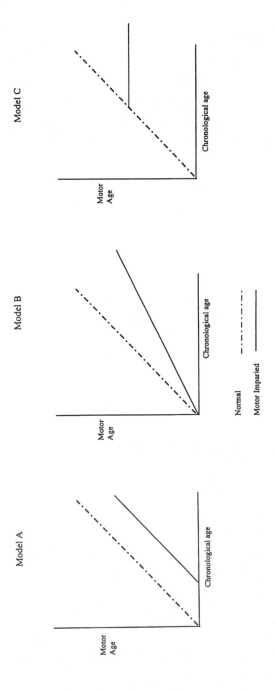

Figure 5.1. Theoretical Models of Motor Development in Motor-Impaired Children
SOURCE: Bishop and Edmundson (1987), adapted and reprinted with permission.

study, Bishop and Edmundson (1987) examined comorbidity of language disorders and hand functions in children, using a peg-board task. Language impairment is associated with poor peg-moving performance, and children with more severe language impairment have more pronounced motor impairment at age 4. The authors explain this clear association between the language and the motor domains as indicators of underlying immaturity and agree with others who regard neuromotor measures as an index of developmental age. The authors argued that the results should be interpreted as neurological immaturity rather than brain damage in that the impairment resembled younger children; it was not static but improved and occasionally disappeared as the child matured.

For disorders of coordination to appear and evolve, complex transactions between biological determinants and environmental opportunities appear to be the salient factors. In the early years, it would seem that certain factors may have both direct and indirect effects. We have already noted the risk and link between low birth weight, short gestational age, and biologically based disorders, such as cerebral palsy. This risk is also linked to other conditions, such as DCD. In addition, there are indirect links because a child with a low birth weight may have a different transaction with a carer who may be reluctant to expose the child to a variety of movement experiences or may provide more protection leading to a poverty of experiences and a small movement vocabulary by the time the child reaches school age. As the child moves through school, the experiences and interventions the child receives are essential to determining the eventual outcome. We have good evidence that developmental disorders of coordination in children are not static nor benign and involve associated risks of lowered achievement, increased behavior disorders, and poorer self-concept (Henderson & Hall, 1982; Losse et al., 1991).

DEVELOPMENT FROM BIRTH TO 6 OR 7 YEARS OF AGE

The relationship between neurological examinations and fundamental units early in life and later behavioral signs at school age has long been a concern of investigators. Several large-scale longitudinal investigations have chronicled the first 5 years of life, examining the progression of those showing at-risk signs at birth to determine the predictive value of certain antecedent conditions. The Collaborative Perinatal Project (Nichols & Chen, 1981) examined these and other variables in a cohort of 30,000 children in the

United States from birth to age 7. Among a number of analyses they conducted was a relative-risk score of including a child in an antecedent or concurrent condition and the probability that child would have a neurological soft sign score at age 7. Sugden and Keogh (1990) prepared some examples from the original Nichols and Chen (1981) data showing, for example, that 811 children in the total sample had very low Bayley scores at 8 months (antecedent conditions). The observed frequency of neurological soft signs in these children was 136 compared to an expected frequency of 70, so giving a relative-risk ratio of 1.95, indicating that children with low Bayley infant scores are 1.95 times more likely to have neurological soft signs at age 7. However, few antecedent or concurrent conditions indicated a doubling of the risk of having neurological soft signs later, and although measures are more predictive the closer they are taken in time, this is not powerful predictive evidence. In a second example, Mutch, Leyland, and McGee (1993) note that the poor performance of low birth weight children on neuromotor tasks is well-documented (Scottish Low Birthweight Study Group, 1992a, 1992b). Motor impairment as assessed by the Movement ABC increased as birth weight decreased, confirming the commonly found motor deficit in preterm low birth weight infants. Mutch et al. (1993) review some of the neuropathological studies searching for a cause and suggest that ischemic insults to the white matter are associated with delayed myelination, which can affect motor behavior.

A major study examining longitudinal data on young children was provided by a developmental screening program conducted by Drillien and Drummond (1983) in Scotland. They were examining the course and occurrence of neurodevelopmental disabilities during the first 3 years of life in relation to educational and behavioral problems during the first 2 years of schooling. The incidence of movement disorders as the primary problem was 1.8% from a stable population of 3,667 children, with additional information available on 100 children who were referred for having movement disorders. Of these, when specialists made detailed assessments for primary disorder, almost 40 could be placed in categories other than the primary disorder. Thus, if the Drillien and Drummond data are typical, prevalence of motor disorders based on screening assessments will be overestimated. An interesting statistic is that 80% of movement disorders were identified early, between 8 and 20 weeks, whereas only around 30% of other problems were identified early. Sugden and Keogh (1990) comment that in the early years, movement behaviors are the prevalent response mode, with the result that movement problems are more likely to be noted, often as indicators of other conditions. The records of the 15 most severe cases were examined for possible causes, with two having perinatal problems, such as anoxia during delivery; six had unknown organic causes identified by four or more congenital anomalies; three had poor home environments; and four had nothing. All of the children had minor neurological signs. All of this points to movement disorders being identifiable early in life, but the causes are neither definite nor similar. In the Drillien and Drummond study, many children with movement disorders also had minor abnormal neurological signs in the first (82%) and second and third (63%) years, but because there was an overall high proportion of children with minor abnormal neurological signs in the first year, having movement difficulties was too common a problem to be a predictor of other problems.

One way to examine etiological factors is to take specific groups of children identified for risk factors and then compare prevalence rates with a control group. This method was used by Hall, McCleod, Counsell, Thompson, and Mutch (1995) who looked at, among other items, motor function of children at 8 years in a population of children who had very low birth weights. Using the Movement ABC (Henderson & Sugden, 1992) as the assessment instrument, the authors found significant differences between both low birth weight groups and control groups. In the children with birth weights of below 1000 g, there were 50% who scored below the 10th percentile on the Movement ABC. In the control group, this figure was 8%. In the children with birth weights between 1,000 g and 1,499 g, there were 34% who scored below the 10th percentile, whereas in their control group, the figure was 11%. Similar results were found by Roth, Baudin, Pezzani-Goldsmith, Townsend, Reynolds, and Stewart (1994) who examined neuro-developmental status at 1, 4, and 8 years of age and found that neuro-developmental difficulties at 1 are good predictors of outcome 7 years later.

Motor coordination disorders have often been included in longitudinal studies that have examined children who have been described under the general heading of *minor neurological dysfunction* (MND). Lunsing, Hadders-Algra, Huisjes, and Touwen (1992a) followed up 3,162 neonates born in the Groningen hospital, Netherlands, between the years of 1975 and 1978. Five percent were found to have a well-defined neurological syndrome, and they were repeatedly compared with matched control groups. The authors hypothesized that incidence of MND would increase up to age 9 and then stabilize, but between 9 and 12 years of age, the incidence decreased. Some children in the original MND group did show decreased dysfunction, and in a subsequent paper, Lunsing et al. (1992b) related this decrease to the onset of puberty and the accompanying hormonal changes, including growth hormones, gonadal hormone levels, and increased thyroxin use. They hypothesized that these would affect strength and possibly decrease hypotonia, and thyroxin may help in neuronal transmission through increased myelination.

Some children identified at birth or shortly afterwards will continue to have motor problems later on. However, individual prediction is difficult. Group data will support the contention that a greater proportion of those with early problems will persist in showing them later in childhood. However, the data are not strong enough to take individual cases and make accurate predictions about future performance. This is made more complex by the measures that are taken at birth. From a group of children with neurological signs at birth, some may not survive; others will develop recognized biological disorders, such as cerebral palsy. From the remainder, there will be a higher incidence of coordination disorders that persist through to school entry, and as we see in the next section, these may go all the way through to adolescence.

DEVELOPMENT FROM 6 OR 7 ONWARD

As we move into an examination of development and progression from 6 or 7 years onward, two types of studies provide us with information from which we can draw out trends and principles. First, there are those studies that focus on a continuation of birth factors and the early years of life. These tend to be large longitudinal studies that examine a number of variables, with motor behavior being one of them. Second, a few studies have specifically targeted motor behavior, usually starting at 6 or 7 years of age and examining a group over a period of time up to 10 years.

General Developmental Studies

Children with various types of disorders are often categorized under a number of headings, and motor coordination deficits are often included in the symptoms. In Scandinavia, the children are often referred for deficits in attention, motor control, and perception (DAMP; C. Gillberg, 1983; Gillberg, Rasmussen, Carlstrom, Svenson, & Walderstrom, 1982), and there may be considerable overlap with conditions such as attention deficit hyperactivity disorder (ADHD) and DCD. In Sweden, children are screened for DAMP at 6 years of age, and many of these children have been followed up over numerous longitudinal studies, and the concept has been shown to be a pervasive disorder with both attention and behavior deficits staying with the children (Gillberg & Gillberg, 1983; Gillberg et al., 1989).

The most comprehensive set of longitudinal studies has been completed by the Gillbergs, who identified children from a whole school population of 3,000 children in the 1980s. They were interested in children with so-called minimal brain dysfunction, attention deficit disorders (ADDs), and minor perceptual dysfunctions. The studies began in the late 1970s, when 7.1% of all children in their cohort had a combination of MPD and ADD and came to be called a *minimal brain dysfunction syndrome* (C. Gillberg, 1983; Gillberg & Rasmussen, 1982a, 1982b; Gillberg et al., 1982). This group is the one that is labeled DAMP in later papers, and to avoid confusion, we shall refer to these children as being in the DAMP group. These children were followed up at 10 years of age and matched with a same-age random sample: 90% of the DAMP group had major behavior and school achievement problems compared to 30% in the control group. However, the neurodevelopmental problems seen when they were 7 had disappeared in 45% of the DAMP group (Gillberg, 1985). In the follow-up at 13 years of age (Gillberg & Gillberg, 1989; Gillberg et al., 1989), the prevalence of behavioral abnormality had decreased substantially to 60% in the DAMP group and a small decrease to around 25% in the control group. The DAMP group still had 65% with school achievement problems compared to less than 8% in the control group.

Using data from the same group, Gillberg et al. (1989) examined neurodevelopmental profiles at age 13 using assessment procedures that included a battery of 13 test items. Both quantitative and qualitative measures were used. In the follow-up from 7 to 10 years of age, the motor problems of 45% of the target children had subsided, and in this study, 6 years after the original study, the motor and perceptual problems had disappeared in 70% of the cases. In their data, they also found that 65% of all children with ADD also had motor and perceptual disorders, thereby arguing for a DAMP category that includes both. The authors noted that the decline in the rates of perceptual and motor difficulties should not be taken to mean that there are no longer any problems, and they suggested that the hard signs of perceptual motor dysfunctions had disappeared but that the underlying problems were still there and emerged in other areas of functioning, such as in behavior and school achievement. A final conclusion from the study was that any child who showed clumsiness was likely to have DAMP or some other neurological disorder.

Hellgren, Gillberg, Gillberg, and Enerkskog (1993), using the same children, examined general physical and psychosocial health 10 years after the original study, at 16 and 17 years of age. They found that children diagnosed as having DAMP at 7 years of age continue to show health problems at 16 over and above those of the general population. The DAMP group had more febrile seizures, more substance abuse, more accidents requiring hospital admission, longer visual reaction times, and a higher rate of gross and fine motor clumsiness. However, although group data showed a higher proportion of problems in the DAMP group, a number of individuals in the DAMP group did relatively well. The authors noted that the presence of minor motor problems, such as increased visual reaction time, together with the disappearance of the more obvious signs of motor dysfunction indicates that DAMP is a neurodevelopmental disorder with changing clinical landmarks but that still continues to cause difficulties throughout childhood and adolescence. They propose this as support for the proposition that motor problems persist in childhood and argue against the notion that children grow out of it.

Michaelson and Lindhal (1993) come to the similar conclusion that even if some children do improve with age, there is still a large group with motor problems. They examined children between the ages of 5 and 9 to determine the background factors to poor motor performance at school age. The risk group of 5.4% of live births was almost 1,200 students born in Helsinki between 1971 and 1974. At 5 years of age, the mean neurodevelopmental score for the risk group was 18.7 and 10.8 for the control group. The value of the motor score from the neurodevelopmental test at 5 years of age was examined for its predictive ability at 9 years. About half the children with high motor scores at 5 had moderate to severe impairment at 9 as measured by the TOMI. The risk group had a variety of neonatal problems, so it was not a homogeneous group. However, 80% of the children had one of three risk factors: less than 2000 g birth weight, hyperbilirubinaemia, or a low Apgar score 5 minutes after birth.

The epidemiology, comorbidity, and overlap of DAMP, ADHD, and other neurodevelopmental or neuropsychiatric diagnostic categories were examined by Landgren, Pettersson, Kjellman, and Gillberg (1996) in 589 6-year-old children. The categories examined were DAMP, ADHD, MPC, cerebral palsy, mental retardation, Tourette's syndrome, autism, and an autistic-like disorder. From the whole sample, 63 children (50 boys and 13 girls) were identified with neurodevelopmental or neuropsychiatric disorders, corresponding to a minimum population prevalence of 10.7%. Using other types of criteria, this figure could be as high as 22%. For individual disorders, the minimum prevalence rates were 5.3% for DAMP, with approximately 9 to 1 ratio of males to females; 2.4% for ADHD and 6 to 1 male to female ratio; 2.5% for mental retardation and 1.4 to 1 male to female ratio; and 1.7% for motor perception disorder with a 9 to 1 male to female ratio. There was considerable overlap across some of the diagnostic categories, so it is not possible to collapse and add up individual rates to find an estimate of the overall prevalence rates. The Landgren et al. study confirmed the general finding from other studies that many neurodevelopmental disorders do exhibit comorbidity as a general feature. In their study, a range of between one in four to three in four of all children with DAMP had ADHD, depending on cut-off signs, and although attention problems were more severe in the ADHD group, overactivity and impulsivity did not differ between the two groups. These large longitudinal data sets examining a number of developmental variables are important for several reasons. First, they provide invaluable descriptions of children with difficulties over long periods of time, allowing us to examine mediating variables that influence the individual's development. Second, and more specific to motor development, they place motor attributes in the context of other development and allow us to examine complex interactions across different attributions. In some of the DAMP studies, if only motor variables had been measured, our knowledge of how difficulties seemingly disappear but reemerge in other areas would have been lost. These studies provide a holistic picture of the child. Last, they allow us to make statements concerning stability, consistency, and change in development. For the specific examination of motor variables, they do have the disadvantage of using different methods to assess the motor domain, they use different terms, and often, the overlap between motor variables and other related ones is difficult to disentangle.

Specific Motor Studies

The difference between what we have labeled *general developmental studies* and *specific motor studies* is not as clear-cut as one would expect. In some studies from the former group, motor abilities do play a major role in the investigation, and similarly, from the latter group, there are other traits and abilities that have been measured alongside the motor ones. However, the emphasis is in the balance, with some studies clearly using the motor domain as just one aspect of development, whereas the studies in this section are examining the motor domain as the primary dependent variable, and other variables are related to the core motor disorder.

The plain-speaking title,"Clumsiness in Children—Do They Grow Out of it?" was used in a unique study by Losse et al. (1991) that investigated the long-term prognosis for children with motor disorders. The authors had originally described a sample of 32 children aged 6, with 16 designated *clumsy* (13 boys, 3 girls) and matched for age, gender, and intelligence with children in the same class at school. Ten years later, they tracked down all 32 children, and information was provided from each of the following: a neurodevelopmental test battery; The Henderson revision of the TOMI; Weschler Intelligence Scale for Children; a Perceived Competence Scale for Children; school records; and interest questionnaire and interview.

The first question the authors asked concerned differences in the motor domain between the original clumsy children and the controls. On the TOMI and the neurodevelopmental battery and from the teachers, there were substantial and statistically significant differences between the two groups, with the control group performing better. When academic achievement and social and emotional status were examined, there was a difference between the groups on verbal IQ, with the controls being superior (100 to 88), whereas at 6 years of age, there was no difference. In school achievement, the controls were much superior despite both groups being given equal ratings for effort. Fourteen out of the 16 controls were taking public examinations, whereas only six of the clumsy group were at this level. From the school records, it was established that the clumsy group had more behavior problems than the control group, some involving police offenses and others involving bullying (see Table 5.1).

The second question that the authors asked concerned the changes within the clumsy group over time. In Table 5.1, taken from the Losse et al. (1991) article, there is a summary of the 17 clumsy children (one extra was inserted after two children originally in footnotes were included—one in each group). The data in this table suggest that the children as a group do tend to have pervasive problems in most areas although there are many individual differences. The scores on the motor assessment instruments show a general lack of proficiency, and there are quite worrying comments from the pupil interviews concerning their experiences and the help or lack of it they received. The authors reported that the academic and social competence scores are more variable, with some adequate, but overall, they are more negative than they anticipated. The sample was too small for an examination of profiles, but they did present case studies showing one child who developed from being quite ·successful at an early age but who at 16 had a very low self-concept and plummeting IQ scores, whose achievement in school was very low, and who had a serious emotional and behavioral difficulty. A second child from the clumsy group still appeared to have motor difficulties, but he had supportive parents and teachers and was still highly motivated to learn new skills. He did not have a low self-concept, his behavior was good, and he was confident. Although his academic achievements were not high, he had many friends and appeared to be a well-adjusted teenager.

The authors discussed some of the more subtle aspects of the question as to whether children grow out of the condition. They noted that in earlier studies, reports of improvement were available, but these reports were beset by difficulties. First, many of the studies were on clinical cases with selected middle-class families who may have had better access to therapeutic

(text continued on p. 91)

TABLE 5.1 Individual Differences Between Children in "Clumsy" Group

TOMI Score	Neurodevel- opmental Test Score	Attainment in Physical Education	Other Motor Problems	Physical Self- Concept	Subject's Own Comments During Interview	Academic Attainment	"Social" Self- Concept	Emotional or Behavioral Problems
1. Very poor	Very poor	Poor	Yes	Poor	I've never been very good at PE and don't like it. I can't coordinate my arms and legs in swimming. I had no help from my teachers.	Poor	Average	Lacks confidence and effort; poor attender
2. —[b]	—	Poor[a]	Yes	—	—	Average	—	Lacks confidence, shy, no friends, has difficulty forming relationships
3. Very poor	Average	Poor[a]	No	Poor	I don't like sports because I'm no good at it. I refused to do it at school. Teachers don't help people like me who are not very good.	Poor	Average	Lacks concentration

(continued)

TABLE 5.1 (Continued)

TOMI Score	Neurodevelopmental Test Score	Attainment in Physical Education	Other Motor Problems	Physical Self-Concept	Subject's Own Comments During Interview	Academic Attainment	"Social" Self-Concept	Emotional or Behavioral Problems
4. Average	Average	Poor	Yes	Poor	I used to be picked last for team games, but you get used to it. You need to persevere, and then you'll get better and enjoy the sport.	Average	Average	None
5. Very poor	Very poor	Average	No	Poor	I couldn't get on in gym, and I avoided PE. You dislike something if you're no good at it.	Poor	Poor	None
6. Poor	Very poor	Average	Yes	Average	I can't play hockey. Rugby is too tough.	Average	Poor	Lacks concentration; forgetful; loner; anxious
7. Poor	Poor	Poor	Yes	Poor	I don't like athletics because I can't run. I don't like gym because I can't do it.	Poor	Poor	Lacks concentration and effort, depressed, easily led astray
8. Average	Poor	Average	Yes	Average	I don't like gym. The vaults are really hard. I can't swim.	Average	Poor	Timid, poor attender, in trouble for stealing

Col1	Col2	Col3	Col4	Col5	Col6	Col7	Col8	Col9
9. Poor	Poor	Poor	Yes	Average	Hockey is too rough. I don't like badminton and cricket.	Poor	Average	Lacks confidence and concentration, lethargic, immature
10. Poor	Average	Poor[a]	Yes	Poor	Football is boring and stupid.	Poor	Average	Depressed, poor attendance, aggressive, abusive, in trouble with police
11. —[b]	—	Average	Yes	—	—	Poor	—	Unreliable, picked on, personality and social problems
12. Average	Poor	Poor	Yes	Average	I don't like athletics, it's too much hard work.	Average	Average	Lacks confidence, quiet, is often absent
13. Very poor	Poor	Average	Yes	Poor	No comments.	Poor	Very poor	Lacks confidence, shy, bullied, muddled, disorganized, plays truant
14. Poor	Very poor	Poor	Yes	Poor	I'm no good at ball games (especially tennis). I'm no good at games and don't get any interest out of it.	Poor	Poor	Lacks concentration, immature, bullied, bizarre behavior

(continued)

TABLE 5.1 (Continued)

TOMI Score	Neurodevelopmental Test Score	Attainment in Physical Education	Other Motor Problems	Physical Self-Concept	Subject's Own Comments During Interview	Academic Attainment	"Social" Self-Concept	Emotional or Behavioral Problems
15. Average	Poor	Poor	Yes	Poor	I don't like cross-country running, it's too tiring.	Poor	Poor	Lacks concentration, lonely, isolated
16. Poor	Average	Average	No	Poor	I dreaded hockey. I don't like the teacher's attitude, she shouted at me. I hated gym because I wasn't good at it.	Good	Poor	Lacks confidence, picked on, bullied
17. Very poor	Average	Poor[a]	Yes	Poor	I can't do PE because I have a false eye.	Poor	Average	None

SOURCE: Reprinted with permission from Losse et al. (1991).

a. In final year, avoided participation in PE; records of earlier years consulted.

b. Not tested, but school records consulted.

intervention. Second, the definition of *improvement* is relatively obscure, and it could simply be a "feeling better" factor. Third, the measurement of improvement had rarely been done using formal standardized assessment procedures. They conclude from their own study that motor coordination disorders are not confined to early childhood because most of the children in their clumsy group still had coordination difficulties into adolescence. In addition, they found pretty conclusive evidence of associated difficulties, including academic achievement, behavior, and self-concept. They were, however, rightly cautious in interpreting these associated difficulties as being direct consequences of motor coordination difficulties as the research methodology did not allow for these conclusions to be drawn. However, it would not be unreasonable to suggest that coordination difficulties in young children should not be ignored because their motor difficulties, without intervention, do not go away and persist into late adolescence, and these difficulties may be strongly associated with other aspects of a child's functioning.

A second 10-year follow-up was reported by Cantell et al. (1994) who examined Finnish children at 15 years who were originally diagnosed as clumsy at 5. At 15, the children were examined for their motor abilities; educational performances; social and emotional development, including self-image; and their leisure activities. Originally, 106 children were identified for clumsiness, and 40 control children were included. At the 10-year mark, a total of 81 of the clumsy children and 34 of the control children were found. Of the 81 clumsy children, 53 were still classified as clumsy, whereas 28 had been reclassified as no longer different from the controls and were labeled *intermediate group.* Of the 81 children identified at 5 years of age, 46% were still significantly different from the control group at 15. The intermediate group had some residual problems, being different to the controls on some tasks and not on others, but their overall performance was better than that of the stable clumsy group. Lower achievement was found in the clumsy group, but this did not become worse throughout the course of the study. Aspirations for their future were also lower for the clumsy group, and they were also quite accurate in their estimations of their performance at school. The clumsy group did not perceive their social status to be any different to other groups, but they took part in fewer out-of-school social activities. The interesting intermediate group did have motor problems at 15, but they appeared to have adjusted to them and were succeeding in educational attainment areas and engaged in social sports and other activities. Cantell et al. (1994) conclude with the statement, "Some children do 'grow out of it;' some do not" (p. 127).

One would estimate that the closer in time identification procedures are, the more agreement there would be. However, even this is not without difficulties. Keogh et al. (1979), in a 2-year study, first asked kindergarten teachers to identify children with motor disorders through the use of a checklist. The selected kindergarten boys were followed through to the first grade where the new teacher also completed the checklist. They also rated a second group of children who had been identified by other means as having motor coordination disorders. Both of these groups were then observed in two physical education lessons by experienced physical education teachers and rated on movement skills, and last, all of the boys were given a five-item movement skill test. Thus, there was the opportunity to examine one group of boys over time using the same identification procedure (checklist) and two groups of boys at one moment in time by different identification procedures. The agreement among the different procedures was not good with kindergarten and first-grade teachers identifying quite a different set of boys using the same procedures. Wright and Sugden (1996b) have argued for a two-step procedure of identification using the DSM-IV (APA, 1994) criteria of serious motor impairment and difficulties in everyday functioning. Children identified by this method would have to show impairments in both of these areas for an identification to be made. The first of these steps is to employ a criterion-referenced instrument, such as the Movement ABC checklist, which is aimed at assessing the child's needs in the school environment, examining every functional task, thus fulfilling criterion B in DSM-IV. The second step is to employ a norm-referenced instrument, such as the Movement ABC test, which can provide normative evidence of serious motor impairment, thus fulfilling criterion A in DSM-IV. This two-step procedure produces a more conservative prevalence figure, but it is more rigorous in that it asks for a demonstration of the disorder across a variety of contexts.

Henderson (1993) noted that until recently, the great increase in longitudinal studies examining the early development of children with motor disorders has been in the age range of birth to 6 or 7 years of age. She focused on a recent series of four sets of studies that have examined development in the 6 to 16 age range. These studies were (a) Dunn, Ho, Crichton, Robertson, McBurney, Buraur, and Penfold (1986) and Dunn, Ho, & Schulzer (1986); (b) Gillberg and Gillberg (1989), Gillberg et al. (1989); and Rasmussen, Gillberg, Waldenstrom, and Svenson (1983); (c) Losse et al. (1991); and (d) O'Connor, Shaffer, Stokman, and Shafer (1986) and Shafer, Stokman, Shaffer, Ng, O'Connor, and Schonfeld (1986). They all labeled their subjects differently and assessed and selected them in different and often idiosyncratic ways. For example, Dunn and associates, using a neurodevelopmental battery, used a numeracy test, with Henderson (1993) questioning the validity of this. On the other hand, Shafer examined so-called soft signs. Henderson, in her analysis of these four studies, does note similarities, including the use of IQ tests, tests of academic achievement, behavior rating scales, and interviews. The children were a heterogeneous group with respect to the severity of their motor impairment and to the extent they had associated difficulties.

The Losse et al. (1991) and Shafer et al. (1986) results for the neuro-developmental examinations were almost identical, with substantial differences at 16 to 17 years of age between the index group and the control group. The Gillberg studies (Gillberg & Gillberg, 1989; Gillberg et al., 1989) had moderately similar results, and in the Dunn studies (Dunn et al., 1986; Dunn, Ho, & Schulzer, 1986), it was not possible to make these comparisons. Social adjustment and school progress was examined in all studies and similar results found, with problems with school work and behavior difficulties persisting in the late teens. When continuity of motor problems was examined with individual children, there was some variability. Shafer et al. (1986) concluded that the neurological test at 7 years is consistently but weakly related to performance at 17 and leading Henderson (1993) to note that the condition does not have a predisposition to fade with age. In the Gillberg studies (Gillberg & Gillberg, 1989; Gillberg et al., 1989), it is noted that 70% of children no longer fail the perceptual motor test, but caution is urged because the tests used may not be appropriate for this age of child, and a ceiling of performance may have been reached. The comorbidity of associated difficulties, such as learning and behavior difficulties, does not go away.

CONCLUSIONS

Motor development is unique among our abilities in that we can measure its progress from birth throughout the lifespan, and the studies we have examined have included such an age range. It is not surprising that if some children have a difficulty early in life, this often continues. We have noted that group data do show this to occur. However, it is also not surprising that some children will change substantially, and difficulties seen at an early age are not seen later, or they appear in a different form.

This chapter has addressed a number of issues that surround the development and progression of DCDs in children. General issues, such as consistency and change, have been related specifically to motor disorders. Two major sections are presented, looking at development and progression from birth to 6 or 7 years of age and from that age to late teens. Very often, these studies do overlap. To obtain any form of individual predication, it is necessary to examine not only the child's performance on various tests but also the ecology of the child's development. How has the condition been recognized, viewed, and managed at home? What support mechanisms have been available at school? What kind of temperament does the child have? What other compensatory abilities does the child possess? These and other questions need to be answered before we start to make accurate predications.

Henderson (1993) obliquely addresses these issues when she discusses the group versus single-case-study approach, and although recognizing the value of the latter, she proposes that longitudinal group data are necessary to examine the multiple variables that influence a child's development. We cannot disagree with this but feel that more single case studies are also essential for more in-depth analysis of the issues. Most disorders, even within a recognized syndrome, are unique and are a result of complex transactions of a number of variables. By an examination of these, we can not only make progress toward more accurate predictions, but we can also prevent predictions with negative outcomes from becoming realities, by effective forms of intervention.

6

INTERVENTION

In his review of intervention strategies for children with ADHD, Hinshaw (1994) notes that treatments have "engendered both consensus and controversy, . . . [and] both investigators and the public appear to vacillate between optimism and pessimism regarding the success of various intervention strategies" (p. 101). With motor coordination disorders, the literature reflects a remarkably similar trend except that research into ADHD has been far more prevalent, with Hinshaw (1994) venturing the proposal that ADHD has had more controlled research than any other childhood disorder. One would hope that theoretical bases and underpinnings of how children develop and learn motor skills would drive intervention and that agreement on these underpinnings would result in consistency of approach. However, this has not always been the case, and we shall outline how the various professions involved come from different perspectives, providing a variety of approaches. A myriad of approaches have been used with children showing motor disorders, and we are not attempting to cover all of them. What we have done is present groups of approaches, with the available evaluation evidence, and at times, introduce our opinions and preferences.

The primary objective of all methods of intervention for children with DCD is to improve their motor skills and their abilities to function in everyday life (Henderson, 1992). There is evidence to show that without treatment of this disorder, the difficulties the children experience persist into later life (Cantell et al., 1994; Geuze & Börger, 1993; Gillberg et al., 1989; Losse et al., 1991) and that the earlier treatment can begin, the better (Schoemaker et al., 1994). More than 25 years ago, Gordon (1969) and Dare and Gordon (1970) acknowledged that children with DCD, who they referred to as clumsy, are in need of special help. They emphasized the need for early recognition and detailed assessment, believing that children not severely affected can be successfully helped, particularly if practice is constant and related to their specific difficulties.

In the first instance, concern for a child with movement difficulties invariably comes from parents or school teachers. Very often, this concern is translated into an investigation by professionals such as the school psychologist and school or family doctor, who may further suggest referral to physiotherapists, occupational therapists, or pediatricians. In the past, difficulties of this nature were often handed over to the appropriate so-called expert in the field with little input from the people who saw the child on a daily basis (Henderson & Sugden, 1992). More recently, the contribution that parents and teachers can make to the intervention process has been recognized (Sugden & Wright, 1995). If a management program is to include the notion of offering help to the child on a "little and often" basis, then there is a strong argument that among the best persons to be involved are the child's parents and teachers. Parents may need guidance in their methods of helping the child with DCD, but as the child's difficulties are evident in the home situation, then the parents are well placed to deal with those difficulties in situ, something that the literature leads one to believe is conducive to improved function (Henderson & Sugden, 1992; Sugden & Wright, 1995; Wright & Sugden, 1997).

Hall (1988), Henderson (1992), Henderson and Sugden (1992), Iloeje (1987), Knight et al. (1990), and Wright and Sugden (1997) have all supported the role of the teacher in the possible treatment of children with DCD. Hall (1988), in particular, states that the treatment should focus on the task causing the problems and remarks that "poor handwriting is not improved by practice in catching a ball" (p. 375). Gordon (1969) suggested that the special help given to children with DCD should concentrate on constant practice linked with adequate motivation provided by teachers and parents. He believed that if the disability is not too severe, then this intervention can be given within the ordinary class in a normal school.

Other professionals involved in the process of helping children with DCD include physical therapists, occupational therapists, music therapists, dance therapists, physical education specialists, and special education teachers as well as the classroom teachers. Referral to specialists outside of the school or home environment, although possibly detracting from help being available little and often and in situ, is often necessary for those children with more severe problems because they provide specialist help (Wright & Sugden, in press). Reports of work involving teachers, by researchers in a clinical setting, and by physiotherapists will be expanded on later in the chapter.

APPROACHES TO INTERVENTION

Individuals involved with the management of children with DCD appear to take two stances toward the intervention. One group, supporting a process-oriented approach, starts from the position that there is a deficiency within the child that needs attention before the child is able to acquire functional skills (e.g., Laszlo & Bairstow, 1985). This deficit is not simply that the child cannot perform the task but involves deficiencies in the psychological processes that are necessary for the task to be successfully performed. These processes include sensory functions, memory, attention, planning, and the formulation of motor programs. The second group, supporting a task-oriented approach, believes that good skill teaching is the route forward, providing the pace is appropriate and the teaching methods are adapted to suit the child (e.g., Henderson & Sugden, 1992). The task is taught more directly, without an emphasis on the underlying processes, but taught in such a manner using a variety of practices so that skill generalization is promoted (Schmidt, 1975). Although these methods, for description purposes, have been proposed as separate entities, they do overlap, occasionally employing similar practices, although for different purposes. Whatever the strategy adopted, the aim is the same: an improvement in the child's everyday functioning. Occasionally, this aim is extended to include other abilities, such as social and emotional development or cognitive development (or both), but the central core aim of most intervention programs contains an improvement in motor functioning.

TASK-ORIENTATED APPROACHES

Principles

Using a task-orientated approach, the personnel managing children with DCD focus on the functional skills that a child is having difficulty with—for example, handwriting. In a very practical way, the supportive aspects of the handwriting tasks are checked and corrected; for instance, the child's posture at the desk is observed and altered, the pen grip adjusted, or the pressure that is placed on the paper as the child writes is increased or decreased as necessary. These aspects are dealt with alongside a simplified program of writing activities, referring back to more basic tasks when needed and building up the motor skills required, little by little. The intervention strategy focuses on the tasks that are causing the child difficulty and link these with the context in which the child is moving.

Within the disability literature, there are programs that have been structured in a task-orientated way, such as the "I CAN" project (Wessel, 1984), where the aim of the teacher is to develop, select, and modify existing curricula to become responsive to the needs of children with movement difficulties. In this instance, the difficulties the children are experiencing represent medically confirmed disabilities. The general approach in the "I CAN" project is to work with functional skills to increase competence through adapting materials after diagnosing the difficulties in the school environment and working with the children within the classroom. There is no preplanned set of lessons waiting to be used, where specific situations fit specific problems; rather, a set of guidelines leads the teacher to ask certain questions and resolve the difficulties by working with the individual child's functional skills in situ.

Cognitive Motor Approach Within the Task Orientation

A comprehensive management plan, especially devised for intervening with children experiencing DCD, is the cognitive-motor approach advocated in the Movement ABC manual (Henderson & Sugden, 1992). The approach involves an eclectic program based on principles derived from the motor learning and motor development literature. This approach involves an analysis of the learning context, which is a complex transaction of the resources of the child, the task to be learned, and the context in which the learning takes place. The approach conceptualizes the acquisition of motor skills as problem-solving exercises, involving the interaction of cognitive, motor, and affective components. Solutions to movement problems are seen as having three main elements: (a) the planning of a motor act, (b) the execution of the act, and (c) the evaluation of the movement. Intertwined with these processes are not only the child's initial perception of the task but also other affective factors, such as the child's motivation, confidence, and interest in improving or learning new motor skills. Incorporating this approach into school-based intervention requires teachers to break down the skills that children are finding difficult and build them up piece by piece, considering the demands of the task and the context in which they are set. The teachers are required to structure the tasks in such a way that there are sources of feedback available to the child intrinsically through movement-related feedback or extraneously from augmented feedback or knowledge of results or both. If the teachers are successful in organizing the learning process as outlined, the child should gain in confidence and become more motivated to continue in his or her endeavors (Henderson & Sugden, 1992). The aim of the intervention is ultimately to get to the stage where the child understands the skill, acquires and refines the skill, and automizes and generalizes the skill. Information from the Movement ABC provides the basis for the intervention. The four motor sections on the checklist deal with functional motor skills in increasingly complex environments, so providing information that starts with skills performed in a less complex environment and moving onto more complex environments. The information from the Movement ABC test is used to confirm and reiterate the findings of the Movement ABC checklist. When implementing the guidelines, the teachers conform to the principle of dealing with the child's difficulties in the context in which they occurred and to working with the child often over short time periods rather than infrequently over long periods.

Henderson and Sugden (1992) believe that analyzing the skills children find difficult by way of these components makes an excellent start to identifying the specific difficulties the children have. They then continue the process with task analysis and task adaptation, thereby linking the assessment of the disorder to the management, with an emphasis on scheduling the management in a meaningful context, which involves practices that are performed in realistic and relevant circumstances. Last, in an attempt to obtain generalization of skills across contexts, they advocate variable practice, that is, using numerous examples of the same kind of task or activity. The cognitive-motor approach is an accumulation and extension of many of the principles gathered from the literature on how individuals acquire more skills, described in the following section.

Motor Learning and the Task-Orientated Approach

Variable Practice: Many of the suppositions and guidelines proposed by Henderson and Sugden (1992) are drawn from the motor learning literature. For example, the idea of variable practice is a practical translation of schema theory (Schmidt, 1975). Through the experience of practicing catching, using many different types of ball, such as sponge balls, footballs, basketballs, or rugby balls, the learner is better able to generalize catching to all newly presented balls, such as tennis balls or baseballs. The theory suggests that a learner acquires a set of rules, a schema, that relates to catching and adjusts the parameters necessary to receive any type of ball thrown toward them. The more experiences that the learner has within a class of events, with different objects arriving from different directions and at different speeds, the more the schema is updated. Variable practice enhances generalizability from experienced tasks to novel situations (Schmidt, 1991).

Timing of Practice: As an aid to variable practice, Henderson and Sugden (1992) urge the teacher to deal with the difficulties the child has little and often. In addition, random practice, a strategy of working on one aspect of movement performance for a short time and moving onto another aspect or different task and then another, rather than blocking the practice, has been shown to be beneficial to the learner with regards to retention of the skill over time. Magill (1989) suggests that random practice requires the learner to be more engaged in the learning process because there is little repetition. Learners are forced into developing more strategies to organize their learning plus have the opportunity to reason and consider more solutions as there is a greater amount of presented problems than in the blocked practice approach. The children are encouraged to become active learners. This has the effect of increasing memory strength, more readily accessed at a later date.

Information and Stages of Learning: Demonstrations, information, and feedback, offered to children with DCD as they practice the tasks they have difficulty with, are essential to learning. The children need to know what to do and how to do it, referred to in the motor learning literature as *declarative* and *procedural* knowledge (Magill, 1989). Many models are presented and are concerned with how information and knowledge becomes organized and structured to provide the basis for a solution to the problem in question. The models suggested in the literature generally incorporate the stage of learning the learner is presently in (Glencross, 1992). Fitts (1964) described three stages or steps of skill learning—a cognitive stage, an associative stage, and an autonomous stage. In the cognitive stage, the child is attempting to understand the task—what it demands and what are the overall objectives. In the associative stage, the child is now in a trial-and-error phase, using feedback from each practice to correct the next attempt. In the autonomous stage, the child can perform the skill without difficulty and without having to pay it much attention—it is automatic. How information and feedback are given to the learner should be linked to the stage of learning. Using Fitts's model of motor learning will influence the presentation of materials and the related issues of knowledge of results and feedback, transfer of learning, and part versus whole learning. Children in different stages of learning need

differentiated help. Just as the blocked versus random practices have produced different effects on practice and learning, differences have been
reported about the effects of feedback on the performance and retention of a
skill (Salmoni, Schmidt, & Walter, 1984). It has been found that if feedback
is offered after each practice trial, performance is enhanced, but retention tests
have shown that this regime of feedback is not the most beneficial to learning.
For increased learning, as opposed to performance, a regime where feedback
is offered initially and then subsequently withdrawn during the practice phase
has been found to be more beneficial. Constant feedback given to the child
while they practice may be of benefit initially but degrades the retention
process as the child becomes reliant on the teacher as a source of information
to correct and detect errors (Wright & Thorpe, 1989). Once the child has been
given feedback, there should be time in which to practice alone. If children
are expected to retain skills over time, they must be allowed to learn to detect
and correct errors independently.

Henderson and Sugden (1992) support the initial breaking down of skills
into simpler parts and the reassembly into a whole progressively to enhance
the learning process. Knowledge of results offers the child information that
can be taken into the next attempt to either rectify or reinforce the skill.
Decoding knowledge of results from either too specific ("that was 3 cm too
far") or too general ("that was too far") feedback into declarative or procedural knowledge can leave the child struggling as opposed to being helped
(Glencross, 1992). If the child is to be actively involved in the learning
process and retain the skill for future use, then the teacher prepares to allow
time for the child to work alone and internalize the parameters and properties
of the tasks being learned. Breaking down the skills children with DCD find
difficult can help in the translation of feedback into declarative or procedural
knowledge. As the skills are simplified and adapted by the teacher, the child
is also better able to practice alone and so strengthen his or her problem-
solving ability and become a more independent learner.

All humans are constrained by their information-processing limitations in
the acquisition of motor skills. Children with DCD display these limitations
more than their non-DCD peers. If skill acquisition can be regarded as the
development of strategies to overcome these limitations, then the cognitive-
motor approach of Henderson and Sugden (1992) through a task-orientated
program seems to offer some solutions (Wright & Sugden, in press). The
methodology involved is to take good practice derived from the models
found in the motor learning literature and apply it to the needs of the children
with DCD.

Evidence of the Effectiveness of
Task-Specific Intervention Programs

The following two studies by Revie and Larkin (1993) and by Wright and Sugden (1997, in press) both make use of task-oriented intervention techniques. Revie and Larkin (1993) selected the children from local primary schools but conducted the intervention outside of curriculum time, whereas the Wright and Sugden (1997, in press) study dealt with the children's difficulties at the schools in which they were originally identified.

Revie and Larkin (1993) identified the children with difficulties through their teachers' completing a checklist designed to select those experiencing movement difficulties and further confirmed the teachers' assessments by use of the Basic Motor Ability Test-Revised (Arnheim & Sinclair, 1979). Once selected, the children took part in a 9-week task-specific intervention program that was incorporated within a program called Uniplay. The children were divided into two treatment groups and taught either the overarm throw and hopping or target kicking and the volleyball bounce and catch. Each group acted as the other group's control. The results of this study revealed that through the intensive teaching of these four skills, the posttest results revealed significant improvements for the overarm throw, target kicking, and the bounce-and-catch task. The children's performance on the hopping task also improved but did not reach significance statistically speaking. The strategy that the teachers took within the intervention program was one where the children could do nothing but succeed, working from simple to complex, and using the whole-part-whole method of teaching. The personalized teaching gave many opportunities for rehearsal and practice of efficient movement patterns. This task-specific approach is very much in line with that advocated by Henderson and Sugden (1992) in practice. In addition, Revie and Larkin (1993) made similar reference to the pragmatism of choosing a task-orientated option when dealing with children who have DCD. Revie and Larkin (1993) stated,

> The task-specific approach has the additional advantage [over the process-orientated approach] of dealing directly with issues of significance to the child. At the end of the program, this was reflected in a mother's comment about her 9-year-old, who "can now skip with a rope and is so happy after years of frustration!" (p. 39)

The children in the Wright and Sugden (1997, in press) study were selected in a similar manner to the children in the Revie and Larkin (1993) report. Teachers in local primary schools completed the Movement ABC checklist in the first instance, and their assessments were confirmed using the Movement ABC test, a battery of motor skills. In this study, the child's teacher, with some assistance from the researcher, attempted to help the child with their specific difficulties during the normal lesson time. Each week, guidelines for the intervention program were prepared, initially by the researcher and subsequently in conjunction with the child's teacher. The guidelines comprised three sections: difficulties seen, action to take, and specific activities. The intervention guidelines were specific to each child's difficulties and worked from the assessment information obtained through the Movement ABC instruments plus the knowledge the teachers had of the children.

Wright and Sugden (1997, in press) report significant differences, in a positive direction, between the pretest and posttest assessments for the children with DCD, with anecdotal evidence from the teachers also available as confirmatory evidence. In both studies, the results demonstrate that task-specific intervention has positive effects for improved functioning of children with difficulties. A major criticism of the Wright and Sugden (1997, in press) study is that the design contained no control group. Thus, it could be argued that any improvement was an attention effect and was not specific to the content of the program. On the other hand, children's individual needs were assessed and addressed, and improvement was significant and specific to those areas directly targeted by their needs assessment. Wright and Sugden (1997, in press) concluded that although teachers are ideally situated to deal with the children's difficulties, the nature or severity or both of the individual child's problems may need the further assistance of movement specialists, such as physical or occupational therapists.

Identifying the factors that contribute to the movement patterns seen in children with DCD is a difficult task, and different perspectives on the organization of movement and movement dysfunction influence the style of chosen intervention programs (Revie & Larkin, 1993). Task-orientated approaches attack the child's difficulties directly, but there are proponents of another approach that chooses to highlight the underlying sensory and other dysfunctions that may account for DCD.

PROCESS-ORIENTATED STRATEGIES

The process-orientated approach does not refer directly to the deficits in functional skills but rather, concentrates on underlying causes that seemingly delay or inhibit the development of functional tasks. This approach has a long history in special education, mainly in the teaching of reading, and the reported varying degrees of success have depended on the program, the processes identified, and the nature of the children (Kavale & Forness, 1985).

Kinesthetic Training

Laszlo et al. (1988) are prominent advocates of process-orientated methods of diagnosis and treatment for children with DCD. Laszlo and colleagues particularly emphasize the role of kinesthesis in the control of movements. Their methods have received much publicity and have generated much debate within the academic community. They have outlined research from the motor learning area plus their own investigations into how children develop their kinesthetic abilities. From this, a process-orientated test, the KST, was developed by Laszlo and Bairstow (1985), which was developed later to produce the Perceptual-Motor Abilities Test to diagnose dysfunction in specific perceptual and motor processes. The diagnosis was used to design kinesthetic training programs aimed at the deficient processes seen in the children with DCD. The results of the training program, as reported by Laszlo et al. (1988), supported their original hypothesis that process-orientated diagnosis and therapy does alleviate perceptuomotor dysfunction (DCD). They state that the significant improvement in motor behavior, as assessed by the teachers of the children with DCD, strongly suggests that kinesthetic process-orientated training generalizes to everyday skills that are different from the training tasks. However, as was discussed in Chapter 4, many researchers have found contrary evidence to that reported by Laszlo et al. (1988), such as Elliot et al. (1988); Lord and Hulme, (1987a); Polatajko et al. (1995); and Sugden and Wann (1987).

The most recent use and duplication of the original work from Laszlo et al. (1988) is reported by Sims et al. (1996a, 1996b). Evaluating Laszlo's approach in the treatment of DCD, Sims et al. (1996a) compared two groups of children with DCD, one group receiving the Laszlo kinesthetic training program, whereas the other group received no intervention and simply attended school in the normal manner. After the intervention program for the treated group, both sets of children were given a posttest. The results showed that both groups had improved on their performances from pretests to posttests, with no differential positive effect seen for the group treated with the kinesthetic training program. Improved function from both groups of children was still evident when the children were again tested 3 months later. In their attempts to reconcile these results with those of Laszlo et al. (1988), Sims et al. (1996a) noted that the method they had used to select and match the children could in itself be deemed to be a form of kinesthetic training and that this procedure may have interfered with their results. To clarify this possible intervening variable, the same set of investigators reviewed their procedures and reported a further study somewhat differently designed (Sims et al., 1996b).

The second study of Sims et al. (1996b), again designed to evaluate the effectiveness of Laszlo et al.'s (1988) work, compared three groups of children with DCD. In this study, one group received the kinesthetic training program, the second group received treatment designed to avoid explicit reference to kinesthesis, and the third group received no training. On this occasion, the selection procedure from the 1996a study that was felt to interfere with the results was not used. The results showed that the two groups who received intervention both improved; the third, untreated, group did not. The results of the second study (Sims et al., 1996b) confirmed the findings of the first (Sims et al., 1996a) in that there was no difference found between the two treatment groups of children with DCD, regardless of whether they received the kinesthetic training program or the program designed to avoid explicit reference to kinesthesis. Sims et al. (1996b) conclude, "It seems that in designing a remediation program for clumsy children, the way that training is presented is as important as its actual content" (p. 996).

This thought is one that Miyahara (1996) also accepts, having completed a metaanalysis of four very different intervention studies on children with DCD. The work of Laszlo and Bairstow (1985) and Laszlo et al. (1988) remain examples of a process-orientated approach to the management of children with DCD, but the original claims made by Laszlo et al. (1988) have yet to be substantiated with the same strength by other researchers. However, it must be noted that the studies by Sims et al. (1996a, 1996b) are encouraging in that they did demonstrate that using the kinesthetic training program resulted in improved function for those children. On the other hand, the studies did not demonstrate improved function over and above the results gained from other methods of intervention.

Sensorimotor Integration Therapy

The work of Jean Ayres (1972) was derived from observations that the environment provides multiple opportunities for our sensory experiences—smell, sight, touch, together with movement and kinesthesis. It is rooted in Piagetian theory with the belief that concrete actions precede intellectual activity, and sensorimotor experiences are the foundations of mental development. It is an approach often used by physiotherapists who work with the child providing multiple sources of sensory input and proprioceptive feedback. It has often been linked to improving subcortical and cortical functioning and is aimed at remediating a number of learning disorders. By an emphasis on tactile, vestibular, and other sensory systems, the therapy is attempting to provide and control sensory input and integrate these into responses. Support for the efficacy of the approach has been provided by Ayres many times in clinical settings, and controlled independent studies, although not differentiating between the effects of sensory integration therapy and other methods, do provide some evidence for its effectiveness. Polatajko, Miller, and Law (1991) found no significant differences between the effects in one group of sensorimotor integration therapy and another group receiving traditional perceptual motor training on measures of reading, writing, fine motor skills, gross motor skills, or self-esteem. In a similar vein, Ottenbacher (1982), after performing a metaanalysis of eight studies, concluded that empirical support exists for sensory integration therapy, but this support is not stronger than for other methods.

Other Sensory Approaches

Baker (1988) took a holistic approach to the assessment and treatment of children with DCD, using both physiotherapists and occupational therapists to run a program of intervention based on psychomotor movements, including muscle power, joint ranges, balance, abnormal muscle tone, coordination, and postural and balance reactions. Activities were chosen that the therapists felt represented the focus of the deficit seen in the assessment; for example, active extension against gravity was encouraged by use of a scooter board or balancing on a large treatment ball. The reported results of the treatment do not include any quantifiable pretest and posttest figures but rather, make statements suggesting that this particular method is beneficial and pertinent to children with DCD. Although functional tasks are used in this type of treatment, the role of the task practice is to encourage the development of an underlying deficit as opposed to becoming accomplished at that specific activity.

Lord and Hulme (1987b) suggested that impairments seen in children with DCD may be accounted for by deficits in basic sensory processes, particularly visual acuity. Their study examined visuospatial perceptual judgments by children and found significant differences between a control group and children with DCD when it came to perceptual processing of visuospatial information, and this would inevitably lead to impaired motor control because correct decisions about appropriate movements could not be made, plus accurate error detection and correction during execution would be hindered.

Lord and Hulme believed children with DCD treated with a perceptual training program would show benefits. Which method of intervention is the most appropriate approach to the treatment and management of children with DCD is a question not easily answered for a number of reasons that we now elaborate on.

ANALYSIS OF INTERVENTION AND MANAGEMENT STRATEGIES

The process of attempting to categorize either an approach to managing DCD or to grouping the children with DCD themselves is not as simple as it may first appear. It is extremely difficult to place people or intervention strategies into discrete groups. The multitude of variables seen in the complex nature of the child's difficulties, the wealth of information thrown up by assessment techniques for DCD, plus the options available on which to base intervention studies all combine to draw researchers into a multidisciplinary approach to the management of DCD, despite the "official" title the approach may don. Even within the process-orientated approach, Sveistrup, Burtner, & Woollacott (1992) acknowledge there are differences as they address the causes as well as the effects of DCD in the design of programs to help these children. They note the heterogeneity of the children with DCD, and although they have identified two approaches to study movement, the systems approach and the computational or modular approach, they accept that several aspects of these approaches are common to both. The same observation can be made of the task-orientated and other process-orientated approaches. The former claims to focus on specific functional skills that are poorly performed, whereas the latter hones in on the underlying causes of the deficit in performance.

Despite what appears to be a clear distinction of approaches at first sight, in practice, these approaches can transpire to similar operational techniques. Adopting the task-orientated approach, a teacher may recognize that a child is having difficulties catching or trapping a ball. The teacher would simplify the learning environment for the child and break down the skills to systematically help the child master catching or trapping, all carried out in context and making use of variable practices. In the case of the child with severe difficulties, the teacher may pare down the movement so that the child begins with balance activities before moving onto any simple ball-related skills. If the child appears to have the supportive fundamental skills, such as balance, in place, then the teacher may simplify and generalize actual ball skills, widening the child's experiences through practices with larger, slower moving balls, rolling a ball before throwing, and so on, gradually building the child's awareness and successes in ball skills. In this case, the teacher has formulated the intervention after witnessing weaknesses in functional skills and has dealt with them in situ.

By comparison, the process-orientated approach adopts the view that the poor task performance is due to an underlying deficit or dysfunctional system that results in poor motor performance and that dealing solely with the task does not discriminate sufficiently to get to the root cause of the child's difficulties. It is argued that identifying the system or computation that is dysfunctional, rather than the skill the child is finding difficult, will allow the development of an intervention program for training the underlying deficit, which will be of greater benefit to more children as they use these underlying systems in a multitude of ways to perform specific skills (Sveistrup et al., 1992). Adopting this approach, it is hoped that the improvements gained will generalize to functional tasks not specifically dealt with. Using a process-orientated approach, the personnel (physiotherapist, researcher, or teacher) helping the child would concentrate on building experiences in the identified underlying cause, which could be the vestibular system, and so work on balance. The overlap of the two approaches now becomes clearer. Working on balance, one would expect to deal with movements that involve both static and dynamic balance, activities such as walking on balance beams, coming to a controlled stop after running, and holding balances on different body parts. Any of these activities could be used to support a process-orientated or task-orientated approach to managing DCD.

Polatajko et al. (1995) compared a process-orientated approach to what they termed a *traditional* or *general motor* approach used by occupational therapists in the treatment of children with DCD. Their major emphasis was to examine the kinesthetic process-orientated approach, but in so doing, they found that when a direct approach to a specific skill was employed, the treatment had a "clear and strong effect" (p. 317).

In spite of the call for a process-orientated approach to intervention, there is a dearth of programs available to deal with children who have DCD. In effect, treatment programs designed for children with other difficulties, such as cerebral palsy or general learning difficulties, are used (Schoemaker et al., 1994). For a teacher in the classroom, the process-orientated approach is a difficult program to operate. The major impediment to adopting a process-orientated approach in schools is the time spent in identifying the underlying causes through laboratory testing, often with expensive equipment. In addition, the noncontextual nature of some of the programs goes against what aids

motor performance (van der Weel, van der Meer, & Lee, 1991). Successes
have been reported by Schoemaker et al. (1994) who systematically monitored the intervention and treatment of children with DCD using a process
based on sensorimotor training dealt with by a physiotherapist in a clinic
setting. The intervention was seen to be effective, with the sensorimotor
training having a positive transfer effect on the untreated skills of a motor
test. The conclusion of the study was that, given an experienced therapist and
an intensive schedule, physiotherapy is an effective method of treating DCD
children. The findings in the Schoemaker et al. (1994) study are noteworthy
for their scientific input and rigor and may be necessary for children with
severe difficulties. However, the practical application of this method on a
large scale would be a very costly affair.

CONCLUSIONS

Despite much work in the DCD area over the years, the emphasis has been
on the identification and assessment of children with motor difficulties, with
a comparative lack of so-called tight research being conducted in the intervention cum management sphere. Knight et al. (1990) reported instances of
help being proffered to children who have DCD and reported improvements
noted in a casual way, leading to a lack of research evidence on which to base
future decisions. Henderson (1992) agrees and notes that there is no definitive
management plan for DCD children with a solid research base. Lansdown
(1988) recommended taking three steps toward helping children with DCD:
first, recognize that help is needed; second, establish the nature of the
disorder; and then third, prepare the program of activities for the management. With regards to the actual management program, he suggests five
ground rules:

(1) It is essential to spend some time on what children can do in order to
maintain their confidence and self respect.
(2) Training or practice sessions should be short rather than long.
(3) Tasks should be broken down into small, manageable steps.
(4) Children should never be hurried; they have their own rate.
(5) Strategies should be taught to overcome specific problems, dressing is a
good example of this. (p. 80)

The approach advocated by Lansdown (1988), including the aforementioned five ground rules, are similar, in essence, to the cognitive-motor
approach suggested by Henderson and Sugden (1992), and they seem to

present a rational and pragmatic starting point for intervention. Miyahara (1996) reminds us, through his meta-analysis of four intervention studies (Laszlo et al., 1988; Polatajko et al., 1995; Revie & Larkin, 1993; Schoemaker et al., 1994), that in appraising the results of these studies, a substantial effect of intervention in general is found, but the differential effect of any specific intervention approach was not supported.

Almost all intervention approaches we have read involve relatively short-term programs using short-term dependent measures. Many of them seem to be successful, yet their long-term efficacy has not been proven. In addition to continuing our search for direct programs that are tightly controlled with all variables highlighted and measured, there may be a place for learning from our longitudinal data and single-case-study data and examining the context of those children who do improve over a period of time. It may be that subtle, small, yet significant changes in the ecology surrounding the child may bring about long-term improvements not addressed by short, controlled intervention studies.

7

FINAL COMMENTS

There are several questions and issues surrounding the topic of developmental coordination disorders in children, and these run across the topics we have delineated as chapter headings. In this final chapter, we will be raising topics that have no specific answers and yet could be seen as the way forward for both researchers and practitioners in the field. Our view on research and practice is that they are not two separate and distinct actions carried out by different personnel but are activities that are interdependent and contribute to each other. Researchers who are developing theoretical principles should and usually do have some practical effect in mind, even if this is long term and the immediate payoff is not obvious. Similarly, practitioners should be and usually are intervening and providing help using some underlying principles for the basis of their work.

A fundamental question to ask is whether or not DCD is a recognizable syndrome that neatly separates itself off from the rest of the population and other disorders. It is often described as a specific developmental disorder, and the same questions are raised as in other specific developmental disorders, such as dyslexia or ADD. Does the syndrome have boundaries around it that are identifiable and recognizable and that logically lead to some form of distinct and different intervention? The alternative to this is that these coordination disorders are simply one end of a continuum characterized by a normal distribution as in other human abilities. One approach to this is to take a middle line that invites criticism of lack of decision making, but this is indicative of the current state of the literature. In research studies and in clinical practice, there are reports of children who appear noticeably different from their peers. Not only are their motor skills poor, but the manner in which they approach situations involving motor skills is often unstructured, illogical, and shows evidence of faulty planning. However, they often show other related disorders, such as personal, emotional, and behavioral difficulties, and in many cases, it is not clear which, if any, is the primary disorder. Very often, there is a suspicion of some undifferentiated underlying problem that gives rise to a number of surface disorders, such as in the concept of DAMP. Other children who have been identified not only show a lower achievement to their peers but also show distinct improvement over a period of years. This raises the issue as to whether permanency of any condition adds to the debate concerning the existence in the first instance of a recognizable syndrome.

We have noted that in many analyses of DCD, the notion of planning is emphasized, and this is particularly the case with the group of professionals who use the label dyspraxia. Planning is also a major issue with other professionals who promote the idea that to perform a skill, one has to know something as well as do something. In other words, in order to execute a skilled action, the person has involved himself or herself in sensory and cognitive planning activities so that successful completion is possible. We are not suggesting that these are distinct and separate actions; in fact, we view them in a dynamic manner, but it is clear that some children do have more difficulties in this part of the skill than in the execution.

This view is taken up by Morris (1997) who separates what she calls developmental dyspraxia into two distinct arenas. The first is the one we have described throughout this book, involving children with DCD or clumsiness. She is quite critical of the literature in this area, noting that definition by exclusion is always hazardous territory and contrasts this with her second area in which childhood dyspraxia is influenced by the adult apraxia models, using gestures as a basis for identification. Although some of her criticism of the DCD literature is unfortunately lacking in substance because of her omission of the longitudinal studies in the area and subtyping in DCD children, her suggestions concerning the field of gestures and learning from adult models are relevant and need to be taken further. She notes that although some test batteries have included imitations of nonrepresentational gestures, they have not been explored as fully as one could expect, and the relationship between developmental motor performance and gestural representation remains largely unresearched. She notes that there is developmental progression in normal children for both representational and nonrepresentational gesture, which is normally complete by the age of 8 years but, with a more fine-grained scoring system, can continue to 12 years of age. In her review of some studies in the DCD field, she also notes that there does appear to be a relationship between poor motor performance and the imitation of gestures, but sound evidence is lacking. She is not convinced that DCD is a separate and distinguishable childhood condition without evidence of other childhood conditions, but she does see a way forward in borrowing more specific assessment items from the study of adult apraxics and using them in a developmental manner. The chapter by Morris (1997) does raise interesting issues concerning the syndrome of DCD. Is it possible that the reason why a definitive syndrome has been difficult to establish is because of the generality or vagueness of most assessment methods together with the extensive range of instruments. In the ones we have outlined, they have either been very specific, such as examining underlying kinesthetic abilities, or are global functional tests, such as the Movement ABC. In both of these, the imitation of gestures is missing, suggesting that the content validity of the test is in doubt. This in turn is related to the definition of the condition in the first instance.

Thus, we are left with these dilemmas. Definitions, characteristics, and nature are intrinsically linked to the assessment procedures and instruments, which in turn are driven by these characteristics. In our article on assessment (Wright and Sugden, 1996b), we tried to move the field on by suggesting that a two-stage procedure was more appropriate than previous assessment procedures, which relied on either a one-off test or a less than reliable clinical observation. We promoted the idea that by employing two different assessment procedures—one, a criterion-referenced checklist and the other, a norm-referenced test—a more stable population of children could be identified. Not only were the two assessment instruments different, but they were often employed by different personnel and in differing contexts. However, as we have noted in our assessment chapter, we are still a long way from having a gold standard assessment instrument. The Movement ABC (Henderson & Sugden, 1992) contains these two instruments, but there are difficulties with both of them, not the least of which is the previously mentioned absence of imitation of gestures. Echoing Morris's (1997) claim, there is probably much to gain by bringing to the developmental area some of the adult literature on apraxia (Rothi & Heilman, 1997). It is only with some recognized and accepted assessment instrument that we can make definitive statements about intergroup and intragroup differences and effectively monitor the developmental progression of the condition through childhood.

One can pursue the line of types of assessment influencing the characteristics and nature by an examination of the difference between clinical samples and large random groups screened from the general population. Smyth and Mason (1997) make the point that their sample of 91 children with DCD selected from 1,277 children in 40 classes may provide different results to a problem-presenting group that has come from a child development center. After the children were selected, using predominantly the Movement ABC,

Smyth and Mason (1997) employed a variety of tasks to examine differences between the selected DCD group and matched controls. These tasks involved an examination of end state comfort using both a handle rotation task and a bar placement task, a task involving nonvisual aiming, matching arm posture, and a kinesthetic sensitivity test. There were no differences between the two groups of children on planning for end state comfort and kinesthetic sensitivity, but there were differences in aiming and posture tasks, leading the authors to observe that in a large group such as this, the DCD children were impaired on some tasks associated with the syndrome but not on others. This rigorous and comprehensive study may be pointing to the method of identification as a major influencing factor when examining the characteristics.

Progression and development of the disorder is very much affected by the methods of identification. We have noted how in some children, the disorder appears to stay with similar characteristics, in others it disappears, and in some, there is still a difficulty but the nature of this difficulty changes. A problem with all longitudinal studies is that over a period of time, the assessment instruments change, and with this change in instrument, even if slight and subtle, we may be focusing on a slightly different group. We have recommended in our chapter on progression and development that case studies over a long period of time would be useful together with more in-depth examinations of group data over a shorter period of time—say, every year for 3 to 4 years and staying with roughly the same assessment instruments, if possible.

The field of intervention is one that is littered with skilled practitioners in both the educational and medical arenas, unproven theories waiting for controlled studies for validation, and a number of guiding principles from the field of motor learning in need of different population groups, which would give generality to these principles that have mostly derived from studies on adult normal groups. We simply do not have enough intervention studies from which to make definitive conclusions. We need more studies, and these new studies need to be placed in a framework that will allow replication and examination with other studies by the use of metaanalyis. The studies need to link intervention to both the characteristics of the sample group and to the principles underlying the intervention procedures. These underlying principles drawn from motor development control and learning and associated disciplines could be the cornerstone of our future approaches to identification, assessment, and intervention.

REFERENCES

American Psychiatric Association. (1987). *Diagnostic and statistical manual of mental disorders* (3rd ed., rev.). Washington, DC: Author.

American Psychiatric Association. (1994). *Diagnostic and statistical manual of mental disorders* (4th ed.). Washington, DC: Author.

Apgar, V. (1953). A proposal for a new method of evaluation of the newborn infant. *Current Researches in Anesthesia and Analgesia, 32,* 260-267.

Arnheim, D. A., & Sinclair, W. A. (1979). *The clumsy child* (2nd ed.). St. Louis, LA: Mosby.

Ayres, A. J. (1972). *Southern California sensory integration test.* Los Angeles: Western Psychological Services.

Bairstow, P. J., & Laszlo, J. I. (1981). Kinaesthetic sensitivity to passive movement in children and adults, and its relationship to motor development and motor control. *Developmental Medicine and Child Neurology, 23,* 606-616.

Baker, J. (1988). A psycho-motor approach to the assessment and treatment of clumsy children. *Physiotherapy, 67,* 356-363.

Bard, C., Fleury, M., Carriere, L., & Belloc, J. (1981). Components of the coincidence-anticipation behaviour of children aged from 6 to 16 years. *Perceptual and Motor Skills, 52,* 547-556.

Bard, C., Fleury, M., & Gagnon, M. (1990). Coincidence-anticipation timing: An age related perspective. In C. Bard, M. Fleury, & L. Hay (Eds.), *Development of eye-hand coordination across the life span* (pp. 283-305). Columbia: University of South Carolina Press.

Barnett, A. (1992). *Manual competence in clumsy children.* Unpublished doctoral dissertation, University of London, UK.

Barnett, A., & Henderson, S. E. (1992). Some observations on the figure drawing of clumsy children. *British Journal of Educational Psychology, 62,* 341-355.

Barsch, R. H. (1967). *Achieving perceptual motor efficiency: A space-oriented approach to learning.* Seattle, WA: Special Child Publications.

Bartlett, F. C. (1932). *Remembering: A study in experimental and social psychology.* Cambridge, UK: Cambridge University Press.

Bernstein, N. (1967). *The coordination and regulation of movements.* New York: Pergammon.

Bishop, D. V. M., & Edmundson, A. (1987). Specific language impairment as a maturational lag: Evidence from longitudinal data on language and motor development. *Developmental Medicine and Child Neurology, 29,* 442-459.

Bruininks, R. H. (1978). *Bruininks-Oseretsky Test of Motor Proficiency.* Circle Pines, MN: American Guidance Service.

Cantell, M. H., Ahonen, T. P., & Smyth, M. M. (1994). Clumsiness in adolescence: Educational, motor, and social outcomes of motor delay detected at 5 years. *Adapted Physical Activity Quarterly, 11,* 115-129.

Capute, A. J., Shapiro, B. K., & Palmer, F. B. (1981). Spectrum of developmental disabilities: Continuum of motor dysfunction. *Orthopedic Clinics of North America, 12,* 3-22.

Clark, J. E., & Phillips, S. J. (1993). A longitudinal study of intralimb coordination in the first year of independent walking: A dynamical systems analysis. *Child Development, 64,* 1143-1157.

Clumsy children. (1962). *British Medical Journal, 296,* 1665-1666.

Connolly, K. (1975). Movement, action and skill. In K. S. Holt (Ed.), *Movement and child development* (pp. 102-110). London: Heinemann.

Connolly, K. (1986). A perspective on motor development. In M. G. Wade & H. T. A. Whiting (Eds.), *Motor development in children: Aspects of coordination and control* (pp. 3-32). Dordrecht, Netherlands: Martinus Nijhoff.

Corbetta, D., & Mounoud, P. (1990). Early development of grasping and manipulation. In C. Bard, M. Fleury, & L. Hay (Eds.), *Development of eye-hand coordination across the life span* (pp. 188-213). Columbia: University of South Carolina Press.

Cratty, B. J. (1981). Sensory-motor and perceptual-motor theories and practices: An overview and evaluation. In R. Walk & H. Pick (Eds.), *Intersensory perception and sensory interaction* (pp. 345-373). New York: Plenum.

Dare, M. T., & Gordon, N. (1970). Clumsy children: A disorder of perception and motor organisation. *Developmental Medicine and Child Neurology, 12,* 178-185.

Developmental coordination disorder [Special issue]. (1994). *Adapted Physical Activity Quarterly, 11*(2).

Dewey, D., & Kaplan, B. J. (1994). Subtyping of developmental motor deficits. *Developmental Neuropsychology, 10*(3), 265-284.

Dorfman, P. W. (1977). Timing and anticipation: A developmental perspective. *Journal of Motor Behavior, 9,* 67-79.

Doyle, A. J. R., Elliott, J. M., & Connolly, K. J. (1986). Measurement of kinaesthetic sensitivity. *Developmental Medicine and Child Neurology, 28,* 188-193.

Drillien, C., & Drummond, M. (1983). Developmental screening and the child with special needs. *Clinics in Developmental Medicine* (No. 76). Oxford: Blackwell.

Dunn, H. B., Ho, H. H., Crichton, J. V., Robertson, A. M., McBurney, A. K., Buraur, V. E., & Penfold, P. S. (1986). Evolution of minimal brain dysfunctions to the age of 12-15 years. In H. G. Dunn (Ed.), Sequelae of low birthweight: The Vancouver study. *Clinics in Developmental Medicine, 95/96* (pp. 249-272). London: Mac Keith.

Dunn, H. B., Ho, H. H., & Schulzer, M. (1996). Minimal brain dysfunctions. In H. G. Dunn (Ed.), Sequelae of low birthweight: The Vancouver study. *Clinics in Developmental Medicine, 95/96* (pp. 97-114). London: Mac Keith.

Dwyer, C., & McKenzie, B. E. (1994). Impairment of visual memory in children who are clumsy. *Adapted Physical Activity Quarterly, 11,* 179-189.

Elliott, J. M., Connolly, K. J., & Doyle, A. J. R. (1988). Development of kinaesthetic sensitivity and motor performance in children. *Developmental Medicine and Child Neurology, 30,* 80-92.

Fitts, P. M. (1964). Perceptual-motor skill learning. In A. W. Melton (Ed.), *Categories of human learning*. New York: Academic Press.

Frostig, M., & Maslow, P. (1973). *Learning problems in the classroom*. New York: Grune & Stratton.

Gentile, A. M., Higgins, J. R., Miller, E. A., & Rosen, B. M. (1975). The structure of motor tasks. *Movement, 7*, 11-28.

Gesell, A. (1988). *The embriology of behavior*. New York: Harper Brothers. Reissued 1988. London: Mac Keith. (Original work published 1945)

Getman, G. N. (1965). The visuomotor complex in the acquisition of learning skills. In J. Hellmuth (Ed.), *Learning Disorders* (pp. 49-76). Seattle, WA: Special Child Publications.

Geuze, R., & Börger, H. (1993). Children who are clumsy: Five years later. *Adapted Physical Activity Quarterly, 10*, 10-21.

Geuze, R. H., & Kalverboer, A. F. (1987). Inconsistency and adaptation in timing of clumsy children. *Journal of Human Movement Studies, 13*, 421-432.

Geuze, R. H., & Kalverboer, A. F. (1994). Tapping a rhythm: A problem of timing for children who are clumsy and dyslexic? *Adapted Physical Activity Quarterly, 11*, 203-213.

Gillberg, C. (1983). Perceptual, motor, and attentional deficits in Swedish primary school children. *Journal of Child Psychology and Psychiatry, 24*, 377-403.

Gillberg, C., & Ramussen, P. (1982a). Perceptual, motor and attentional deficits in six year old children: Screening procedures in pre-school. *Acta Paediatrica Scandinavia, 71*, 121-129.

Gillberg, C., & Rasmussen, P. (1982b). Perceptual, motor and attentional deficits in seven year old children: Background factors. *Developmental Medicine and Child Neurology, 24*, 752-770.

Gillberg, C., Rasmussen, P., Carlstrom, G., Svenson, B., & Waldenstrom, E. (1982). Perceptual, motor and attentional deficits in six year old children: Epidemiological aspects. *Journal of Child Psychology and Psychiatry, 23*, 131-144.

Gillberg, I. C. (1985). Children with minor neurodevelopmental disorders: Part 3: Neurological and neurodevelopmental problems at age 10. *Developmental Medicine and Child Neurology, 27*, 3-16.

Gillberg, I. C., & Gillberg, C. (1983). Three year follow up at age 10 of children with minor neurodevelopmental disorders: Part 1. Behavioral problems. *Developmental Medicine and Child Neurology, 25*, 438-449.

Gillberg, I. C., & Gillberg, C. (1989). Children with preschool minor neurodevelopmental disorders: Part 4. Behaviour and school achievement at age 13. *Developmental Medicine and Child Neurology, 31*, 3-13.

Gillberg, I. C., Gillberg, C, & Groth, J. (1989). Children with preschool minor neurodevelopmental disorders: Neurodevelopmental profiles at age 13. *Developmental Medicine and Child Neurology, 31*, 14-24.

Glencross, D. J. (1992). Human skill and motor learning: A critical review. *Sport Science Review, 1*, 65-78.

Gordon, N. (1969). Helping the clumsy child in school. *Special Education, 58*, 19-20.

Griffiths, R. (1970). *The abilities of young children: A comprehensive system of mental measurement for the first eight years of life*. London: Child Development Research Centre.

Gubbay, S. S. (1975a). Clumsy children in normal schools. *Medical Journal of Australia,* *1,* 233-236.

Gubbay, S. S. (1975b). *The clumsy child.* Philadelphia: Saunders.

Hall, A., McCleod, A. Counsell, C., Thompson, L., & Mutch, L. (1995). School attainment, cognitive ability and motor function in a Scottish very low birthweight population at eight years: A controlled study. *Developmental Medicine and Child Neurology, 37,* 1037-1050.

Hall, D. M. B. (1988). Clumsy children. *British Medical Journal, 296,* 375-376.

Hay, L. (1979). Spatial temporal analysis of movements in children: Motor programmes versus feedback in the development of reaching. *Journal of Motor Behavior, 11,* 189-200.

Hay, L. (1990). Developmental changes in eye-hand coordination behaviors: Preprogramming versus feedback control. In C. Bard, M. Fleury, & L. Hay (Eds.), *Development of eye-hand coordination across the lifespan* (pp. 217-244). Columbia: University of South Carolina Press.

Hellgren, L., Gillberg, C., Gillberg, I. C., & Enerkskog, I. (1993). Children with deficits in attention, motor control and perception (DAMP) almost grown up: General health at 16 years. *Developmental Medicine and Child Neurology, 35,* 881-892.

Henderson, L., Rose, P., & Henderson, S. E. (1992). Reaction time and movement time in children with a developmental coordination disorder. *Journal of Child Psychology and Psychiatry, 33,* 895-905.

Henderson, S. E. (1987). The assessment of 'clumsy children': Old and new approaches. *Journal of Child Psychology and Psychiatry, 28,*(4), 511-527.

Henderson, S. E. (1992). Clumsiness or developmental coordination disorder: A neglected handicap. *Current Paediatrics, 2,* 158-162

Henderson, S. E. (1993). Motor development and minor handicap. In A. F. Kalverboer, B. Hopkins, & R. Geuze (Eds.), *Motor development in early and later childhood: Longitudinal approaches* (pp. 286-306). Cambridge, UK: Cambridge University Press.

Henderson, S. E. (1994). Editorial. *Adapted Physical Activity Quarterly, 11,* 111-114.

Henderson, S. E., & Hall, D. (1982). Concomitants of clumsiness in young children. *Developmental Medicine and Child Neurology, 24,* 448-460.

Henderson, S. E., May, D. S., & Umney, M. (1989). An exploratory study of goal-setting behaviour, self-concept and locus of control in children with movement difficulties. *European Journal of Special Needs Education, 4,* 1-13.

Henderson, S. E., & Sugden, D. A. (1991). Signposts to special needs: Pupils with motor impairment. *National Children's Bureau.* Nottingham, UK: Nes Arnold.

Henderson, S. E., & Sugden, D. A. (1992). *Movement assessment battery for children.* London: Psychological Corporation.

Hinshaw, S. P. (1994). *Attention deficits and hyperactivity in children.* Thousand Oaks, CA: Sage.

Hoare, D. (1991). *Classification of movement dysfunctions in children: Descriptive and statistical approaches.* Unpublished doctoral dissertation, University of Western Australia, Perth, Australia.

Hoare, D. (1994). Subtypes of developmental coordination disorder. *Adapted Physical Activity Quarterly, 11,* 158-169.

Hulme, C., Biggerstaff, A., Moran, G., & McKinlay, I. (1982). Visual, kinaesthetic and cross-modal judgements of length by normal and clumsy children. *Developmental Medicine and Child Neurology, 24,* 461-471.

Hulme, C., & Lord, R., (1986). Clumsy children: A review of recent research. *Child: Care, Health and Development, 122,* 256-269.

Hulme, C., Smart, A., & Moran, G. (1982). Visual perceptual deficits in clumsy children. *Neuropsychologia, 20,* 475-481.

Hulme, C., Smart, A., Moran, G., & McKinlay, I. (1984). Visual, kinaesthetic and cross-modal judgements of length by clumsy children: A comparison with young normal children. *Child: Care, Health and Development, 10,* 117-125.

Iloeje, S. O. (1987). Developmental apraxia among Nigerian children in Enugu, Nigeria. *Developmental Medicine and Child Neurology, 29,* 502-507.

Jeannerod, M. (1988). *The neural and behavioural organization of goal-directed movements.* New York: Oxford University Press.

Kalverboer, A. F., De Vries, H., & van Dellen, T. (1990). Social behaviour in clumsy children as rated by parents and teachers. In A. F. Kalverboer (Ed.), *Developmental biopsychology: Experimental and observational studies in children at risk* (pp. 257-270). Ann Arbor: University of Michigan Press.

Kavale, K. A., & Forness, S. R. (1995). *The nature of learning disabilities.* Hillsdale, NJ: Lawrence Erlbaum.

Kellogg, R., & O'Dell, S. (1969). *Analyzing children's art.* Palo Alto, CA: National Press Books.

Kelso, J. A. S., & Tuller, B. (1984). A dynamical basis for action systems. In M. S. Gazzaniga (Ed.), *Handbook of cognitive neuroscience* (pp. 321-356). New York: Plenum.

Keogh, J. F., & Sugden, D. A. (1985). *Movement skill development.* New York: Macmillan.

Keogh, J. F., Sugden, D. A., Reynard, C. L., & Calkins, J. A. (1979). Identification of clumsy children: Comparisons and comments. *Journal of Human Movement Studies, 5,* 32-41.

Kephart, N. C. (1960). *The slow learner in the classroom.* Columbus, OH: Merrill.

Knight, E., Henderson, S. E., Losse, A., & Jongmans, M. (1990, July). Clumsy at six—Still clumsy at sixteen: The educational and social consequences of having motor difficulties at school. *Proceedings of the AIESEP World Convention,* Loughborough University, UK.

Kugler, P., & Turvey, M.T. (1987). *Information, natural law, and the self assembly of rhythmic movement.* Hillsdale, NJ: Lawrence Erlbaum.

Kugler, P. N. (1986). A morphological perspective on the origin and evolution of movement patterns. In M. G. Wade & H. T. S. Whiting (Eds.), *Motor development in children: Aspects of coordination and control* (pp. 459-525). Dordrecht, Netherlands: Martinus Nijhoff.

Landgren, M., Pettersson, R., Kjellman, B., & Gillberg, C. (1996). ADHD, DAMP and other neurodevelopmental/psychiatric disorders in 6 year old children: Epidemiology and co-morbidity. *Developmental Medicine and Child Neurology, 38,* 891-906.

Langendorfer, S. (1986). Test of Motor Development; D. A. Ulrich: A review. *Adapted Physical Activity Quarterly, 3,* 186-190.

Lansdown, R. (1988). The clumsy child. In N. Richman & R. Lansdown (Eds.), *Problems of preschool children* (pp. 75-82). London, UK: Wiley.

Larkin, D., & Hoare, D. (1992). The movement approach: A window to understanding the clumsy child. In J. J. Summers (Ed.), *Approaches to the study of motor control and learning* (pp. 413-439). Amsterdam: North Holland.

Lassner, R. (1948). Annotated bibliography on the Oserestsky tests of motor proficiency. *Journal of Consulting Psychology, 12,* 37-47.

Laszlo, J. I., & Bairstow, P. J. (1980). The measurement of kinaesthetic sensitivity in children and adults. *Developmental Medicine and Child Neurology, 22,* 254-464.

Laszlo, J. I., & Bairstow, P. J. (1983). Kinaesthesis: Its measurement, training and relationship to motor control. *Quarterly Journal of Experimental Psychology, 35,* 411-421.

Laszlo, J. I., & Bairstow, P. J. (1985). *Perceptual-motor behaviour: Development assessment and therapy.* London: Holt, Rinehart & Winston.

Laszlo, J. I., Bairstow, P. J., Bartrip, J., & Rolfe, V. T. (1988). Clumsiness or perceptuomotor dysfunction? In A. Colley & J. Beech (Eds.), Cognition and action in skilled behaviour (pp. 293-316). Amsterdam: North Holland.

Latash, M. L. (1993). *Control of human movement.* Champaign, IL: Human Kinetics.

Leavitt, J. L. (1979). Cognitive demands of skating and stick handling in ice hockey. *Canadian Journal of Applied Sports Sciences, 4,* 46-55.

Lockman, J. J., & Thelen, E. (1993). Developmental biodynamics: Brain, body, behavior connections. *Child Development, 64,* 953-959.

Lord, R., & Hulme, C. (1987a). Kinaesthetic sensitivity of normal and clumsy children. *Developmental Medicine and Child Neurology, 29,* 720-725.

Lord, R., & Hulme, C. (1987b). Perceptual judgment of normal and clumsy children. *Developmental Medicine and Child Neurology, 29,* 250-257.

Lord, R., & Hulme, C. (1988). Patterns of rotary pursuit performance in clumsy and normal children. *Journal of Child Psychology and Psychiatry, 29,* 691-701.

Losse, A., Henderson, A. E., Elliman, D., Hall, D., Knight, E., & Jongmans, M. (1991). Clumsiness in children—Do they grow out of it? A ten-year follow-up study. *Developmental Medicine and Child Neurology, 33,* 55-68.

Lundy-Ekman, L., Ivry, R., Keele, S., & Woollacott, M. (1991). Timing and force control deficits in clumsy children. *Journal of Cognitive Neuroscience, 3(4),* 367-376.

Lunsing, R. J., Hadders-Algra, M., Huisjes, H. J., & Touwen, B. C. L. (1992a). Minor neurological dysfunction from birth to 12 years: Increase during late school-age. *Developmental Medicine and Child Neurology, 34,* 399-403.

Lunsing, R. J., Hadders-Algra, M., Huisjes, H. J., & Touwen, B. C. L. (1992b). Minor neurological dysfunction from birth to 12 years: 11. Puberty is related to decreased dysfunction. *Developmental Medicine and Child Neurology, 34,* 404-409.

Lyytinen, H., & Ahonen, T. (1989). Motor precursors of learning disabilities. In D. J. Bakker & H. Vlugt (Eds.), *Learning Disabilities: Vol. 1. Neuro-psychological correlates* (pp. 35-43). Amsterdam: Swets & Zeitlinger.

Maeland, A. F. (1992). Identification of children with motor coordination problems. *Adapted Physical Activity Quarterly, 9,* 330-342.

Magill, R. A. (1989). *Motor learning concepts and applications.* Dubuque, IA: Brown.

Manoel, E. J., & Connolly, K. (1997). Variability and stability in the development of the human infant. In K. J. Connolly, & H. Forssberg (Eds.), *Neurophysiology and neuropsychology of motor development* (pp. 286-318). London: Mac Keith.

McClenaghan, B. A., & Gallahue, D. C. (1978). Fundamental movement: A developmental and remedial approach. Philadelphia: Saunders.

McGovern, R. (1991). Developmental dyspraxia: Or just plain clumsy? *Early years, 12*, 37-38.

McGraw, M. B. (1946). Maturation of behavior. In L. Carmichael (Ed.), *Manual of child psychology* (pp. 354-361). New York: John Wiley.

McGraw, M. B. (1963). *The neuromuscular maturation of the human infant* (Reprint ed.). New York: Hafner.

Michelson, K., & Lindahl, E. (1993). Relationship between perinatal risk factors and motor development at the ages of 5 and 9 years. In A. F. Kalverboer, B. Hopkins, & R. Geuze (Eds.), *Motor development in early and later childhood: Longitudinal approaches* (pp. 266-285). Cambridge, UK: Cambridge University Press.

Missiuna, C. (1994). Motor skill acquisition in children with developmental coordination disorder. *Adapted Physical Activity Quarterly, 11*, 214-235.

Miyahara, M. (1996). A meta-analysis of intervention studies on children with Developmental Coordination Disorder. *Corpus, Psyche et Societas, 3*, 11-18.

Mon-Williams, M. A., Wann, J. P., & Pascal, E. (1994). Ophthalmic factors in developmental coordination disorder. *Adapted Physical Activity Quarterly, 11*, 170-178.

Morris, M. K. (1997). Developmental dyspraxia. In L. J. G. Rothi & K. M. Heiman (Eds.), *Apraxia: The neuropsychology of action* (pp. 245-268). Hove, East Sussex, UK: Psychology Press.

Morris, P. R., & Winter, P. M. (1975). Identifying clumsy children. *Research Papers in Physical Education, 3*, 4-8.

Murphy, J. B., & Gilner, J. A. (1988). Visual and motor sequencing in normal and clumsy children. *Occupational Therapy Journal of Research, 8*, 89-103.

Mutch, L., Leyland, A., & McGee, A. (1993). Patterns of neuropsychological function in a low-birthweight population. *Developmental Medicine and Child Neurology, 35*, 943-956.

Nichols, P. L., & Chen, T. C. (1981). *Minimal brain dysfunction: A prospective study.* Hillsdale, NJ: Lawrence Erlbaum.

O'Beirne, C., Larkin, D., & Cable, T. (1994). Coordination problems and anaerobic performance in children. *Adapted Physical Activity Quarterly, 11*, 141-149.

O'Connor, P., Shaffer, D., Stokman, C., & Shafer, S. Q. (1986). A neuro-psychiatric follow-up of children in the Collaborative Perinatal Project: A longitudinal study of neurological signs in childhood. In S. Mednick & M. Hanway (Eds.), *Longitudinal research in the United States* (pp. 108-117). New York: Praeger.

Ottenbacher, K. (1982). Sensory integration therapy: Affect or effect. *American Journal of Occupational Therapy, 36*, 571-578.

Polatajko, H. J., MacNab, J. J., Anslett, B. Malloy-Miller, T., Murphy, K., & Noh, S. (1995). A clinical trial of the process-orientated-treatment approach for children with developmental coordination disorder. *Developmental Medicine and Child Neurology, 27*, 310-319.

Polatajko, H. J., Miller, J., & Law, M. (1991). The effect of a sensory integration theory program on academic achievement, motor performance and self esteem in children identified as learning difficulties: Results of a clinic trial. *American Occupational Therapy Journal of Research, 9*, 155-176.

Rasmussen, P., Gillberg, C., Waldenstrom, E., & Svenson, B. (1983). Perceptual, motor and attentional deficits in seven-year-old children: Neurological and neurodevelopmental aspects. *Developmental Medicine and Child Neurology, 25*, 315-333.

Revie, G., & Larkin, D. (1993). Task-specific intervention with children reduces movement problems. *Adapted Physical Activity Quarterly, 10,* 29-41.

Rösblad, B., & von Hofsten, C. (1994). Repetitive goal-directed arm movements in children with Developmental Coordination Disorders: Role of visual information. *Adapted Physical Activity Quarterly, 11,* 190-202.

Rosenbaum, D. A. (1991). *Human motor control.* New York: Academic Press.

Roth, S. C., Baudin, J., Pezzani-Goldsmith, M., Townsend, J., Reynolds, E. O. R., & Stewart, A. L. (1994). Relation between neurodevelopmental status of very preterm infants at one and eight years. *Developmental Medicine and Child Neurology, 36,* 1049-1062.

Rothi, L. J. G, & Heilman, K. M. (Eds.). (1997). *Apraxia: The neuropsychology of action.* Hove, East Sussex, UK: Psychology Press.

Roussounis, S. H., Gaussen, T. H., & Stratton, P. (1987). A 2-year follow up of children with motor coordination problems identified at school entry age. *Child: Care, Health and Development, 13,* 377-391.

Rutter, M. (1989). Pathways from childhood to adult life. *Journal of Child Psychology and Psychiatry, 30*(1), 23-51.

Salmoni, A. W., Schmidt, R. A., & Walter, C. B. (1984). Knowledge of results and motor learning: A review and critical appraisal. *Psychological Bulletin, 3,* 355-386.

Schmidt, R. A. (1975). A schema theory of discrete motor skill learning. *Psychological Review, 82,* 225-260.

Schmidt, R. A. (1988). *Motor control and learning* (2nd ed.). Champaign, IL: Human Kinetics.

Schmidt, R. A. (1991). *Motor learning and performance: From principles to practice.* Champagne, IL: Human Kinetics.

Schoemaker, M. M., Hijklema, M. G. J., & Kalverboer, A. F. (1994). Physiotherapy for clumsy children: An evaluation study. *Developmental Medicine and Child Neurology, 36,* 143-155.

Schoemaker, M. M., & Kalverboer, A. F. (1994). Social and affective problems of children who are clumsy: How early do they begin? *Adapted Physical Activity Quarterly, 11,* 130-140.

Scottish Low Birthweight Study Group. (1992a). The Scottish low birthweight study: 1. Survival, growth and physical impairment at four years. *Archives of Disease in Childhood, 67,* 675-681.

Scottish Low Birthweight Study Group. (1992b). The Scottish Low Birthweight Study: 2. Language attainment, cognitive status and behavioural problems at four years. *Archives of Disease in Childhood, 67,* 682-686.

Shafer, S. Q., Stokman, C. J., Shaffer, D., Ng, S. K. C., O'Connor, P. A., & Schonfield, I. S. (1986). Ten-year consistency in neurological test performance of children without focal neurological deficit. *Developmental Medicine and Child Neurology, 28,* 417-427.

Shaw, L., Levine, M. D., & Belfer, M. (1982). Developmental double jeopardy: A study of clumsiness and self-esteem in children with learning problems. *Developmental and Behavioural Pediatrics, 3,* 191-196.

Shea, C. H., Krampitz, J. B., Northam, C. C., & Ashby, A. A. (1982). Information processing coincident timing tasks: A developmental perspective. *Journal of Human Movement Studies, 8,* 73-83.

Silva, P. A., & Ross, B. (1980). Gross motor development and delays in development in early childhood: Assessment and significance. *Journal of Human Movement Studies, 6,* 211-226.

Sims, K., Henderson, S. E., Hulme, C., & Morton, J. (1996a). The remediation of clumsiness: 1. An evaluation of Laszlo's kinaesthetic approach. *Developmental Medicine and Child Neurology, 38*(11), 976-987.

Sims, K., Henderson, S. E., Morton, J., & Hulme, C. (1996b). The remediation of clumsiness: 2. Is kinaesthesis the answer? *Developmental Medicine and Child Neurology, 38*(11), 988-997.

Skorji, V., & McKenzie, B. (1997). How do children who are clumsy remember modelled movements? *Developmental Medicine and Child Neurology, 39,* 404-408.

Smyth, M. M., & Mason, U. C. (1997). Planning and execution of action in children with and without developmental coordination disorder. *Journal of Child Psychology and Psychiatry, 38*(3), 1023-1037.

Smyth, T. R., & Glencross, D. J. (1986). Information processing deficits in clumsy children. *Australian Journal of Psychology, 38,* 13-22.

Spaeth-Arnold, R. K. (1981). Developing sport skills. *Motorskills: Theory into practice* (Monograph 2). Bronx, NY: Herbert H. Lehman College, DHPER Department.

Sporns, O., & Edelman, G. M. (1993). Solving Bernstein's problem: A proposal for the development of coordinated movement by selection. *Child Development, 64,* 960-981.

Stanley, F. (1984). Prenatal risk factors in the study of the cerebral palsies. In F. Stanley & E. Alberman, (Eds.), *The epidemiology of the cerebral palsies* (pp. 87-97). London: Spastics International.

Stanley, F., & Alberman, E. (1984). Birthweight, gestational age and the cerebral palsies. In F. Stanley & E. Alberman (Eds.), *The epidemiology of the cerebral palsies* (pp. 135-149). London: Spastics International.

Stott, D. H., Moyes, F. A., & Henderson, S. E. (1984). *The test of motor impairment— Henderson revision.* San Antonio, TX: The Psychological Corporation.

Sugden, D. A. (1972). *Incidence and nature of motoric problems and related behaviours in kindergarten children.* Unpublished master's degree thesis, University of California, Los Angeles.

Sugden, D. A. (1990). Role of proprioception in eye-hand coordination. In C. Bard, M. Fleury, & L. Hay (Eds.), *Development of eye-hand coordination across the lifespan* (pp. 133-153). Columbia: University of South Carolina Press.

Sugden, D. A., & Henderson, S. E. (1994). Back to basics: Help with movement. *Special Children, 75.*

Sugden, D.A., & Keogh, J. F. (1990). *Problems in movement skill development.* Columbia: University of South Carolina Press.

Sugden, D. A., & Sugden, L. (1991). The assessment of movement skill problems in 7 and 9 year old children. *British Journal of Educational Psychology, 61,* 329-345.

Sugden, D., & Wann, C. (1987). The assessment of motor impairment in children with moderate learning difficulties. *British Journal of Educational Psychology, 57,* 225-236.

Sugden, D. A., & Wright, H. C. (1995). *Helping your child with movement difficulties.* Leeds, UK: Harmers.

Sugden, D. A., & Wright, H. C. (1996). Curricular entitlement and implementation for all children. In N. Armstrong (Ed.), *New directions in physical education: Vol. 3. Change and innovation* (pp. 110-130). London: Cassells.

Sveistrup, H., Burtner, P. A., & Woollacott, M. H. (1992). Two motor control approaches that may help to identify and teach children with motor impairments. *Pediatric Exercise Science, 4,* 249-269.

Thelen, E. (1995). Motor development: A new synthesis. *American Psychologist, 50*(2), 79-95.

Touwen, B. C. L. (1979). Examination of the child with minor neurological dysfunction. *Clinics in Developmental Medicine, No. 71.* London: S.I.M.P./Heinemann.

Turvey, M. T. (1990). Coordination. *American Psychologist, 45,* 938-953.

Turvey, M. T., & Fitzpatrick, P. (1993). Commentary: Development of perception-action systems and general principles of pattern formation. *Child Development, 64,* 1175-1190.

Ulrich, B. D. (1997). Dynamic systems theory and skill development in infants and children. In K.J. Connolly, & H. Forssberg (Eds.), *Neurophysiology and neuropsycholoy of motor development* (pp. 319-345). London: Mac Keith Press.

Ulrich, D. (1985). *Test of gross motor development.* Austin, TX: Pro-Ed.

Vaessen, W., & Kalverboer, A. F. (1990). Clumsy children's performance on a double task. In A. F. Kalverboer (Ed.), *Developmental biopsychology: Experimental and observational studies in children at risk* (pp. 223-240). Ann Arbor: University of Michigan Press.

van Dellen, T., & Geuze, R. H. (1988). Motor response processing in clumsy children. *Journal of Child Psychology and Psychiatry, 29,* 489-500.

van Dellen, T., & Geuze, R. H. (1990). Experimental studies in motor control in clumsy children. In A. F. Kalverboer (Ed.), *Developmental biopsychology: Experimental and observational studies in children at risk* (pp. 187-205). Ann Arbor: University of Michigan Press.

van Dellen, T., Vaessen, W., & Schoemaker, M. M. (1990). Clumsiness: Definition and selection of subjects. In A. F. Kalverboer (Ed.), *Developmental biopsychology: Experimental and observational studies in children at risk* (pp. 135-152). Ann Arbor: University of Michigan Press.

van der Meulen, J. H. P., Denier van der Gon, J. J., Geilen, C. C. A. M., Gooskens, R. H. J. M., & Willemse, J. (1991). Visuomotor performance of normal and clumsy children: 2. Arm-tracking with and without visual feedback. *Developmental Medicine and Child Neurology, 33,* 118-129.

van der Weel, F. R., van der Meer, A. L. H., & Lee, D. N. (1991). Effect of task on movement control in cerebral palsy: Implications for assessment and therapy. *Developmental Medicine and Child Neurology, 33,* 419-426.

Vereijken, B., Whiting, H. T. A., & Beek, W. (1992). A dynamical systems approach to skill learning. In G. E. Stemach & J. Requin (Eds.), *Tutorials in motor behavior* (pp. 225-236). Amsterdam: North Holland.

Von Hofsten, C.(1980). Predictive reaching for moving objects by human infants. *Journal of Experimental Child Psychology, 30,* 369-382.

Waddington, C. H. (1957). *The strategy of the genes.* London: George Allen & Unwin.

Wade, M. J. (1980). Coincidence anticipation of young normal and handicapped children. *Journal of Motor Behavior, 12*, 103-112.

Walton, J. N., Ellis, E., & Court, S. D. M. (1962). Clumsy children: Developmental apraxia and agnosia. *Brain, 85*, 603-612.

Wann, J. P. (1986). Handwriting disturbances: Developmental trends. In H. T. A. Whiting & M. G. Wade (Eds.), *Themes in Motor Development* (pp. 207-223). Dordrecht, Netherlands: Martinus Nijhoff.

Wann, J. P. (1987). Trends in the refinement and optimization of fine-motor trajectories: Observations from an analysis of the handwriting of primary school children. *Journal of Motor Behavior, 19*, 13-37.

Wessel, J. (1984). The "I can" project: A perspective. In A. Brown, D. Brickell, L. Groves, E. McLeish, & D. Sugden (Eds.), *Adaptive physical activities* (pp. 146-157). UK: Jenny Lee Publishing Services.

Whiting, H. T. A., Clarke, T. A., & Morris, P. R. (1969). A clinical validation of the Stott Test of Motor Impairment. *British Journal of Social and Clinical Psychology, 8*, 270-274.

Williams, H. G., & Burke, J. R. (1995). Conditioned patellar tendon reflex function in children with and without developmental coordination disorders. *Adapted Physical Activity Quarterly, 12*, 250-261.

World Health Organization. (1992a). *International statistical classification of diseases and related health problems* (10th ed., Vol. 1). Geneva, Switzerland: Author.

World Health Organization. (1992b). *Classification of mental and behavioural disorders: Clinical descriptions and diagnostic guidelines*. Geneva, Switzerland: Author.

World Health Organization. (1993). *Classification of mental and behavioural disorders: Diagnostic criteria for research*. Geneva, Switzerland: Author.

Wright, H. C. (1996). *The identification, assessment and management of children with developmental coordination disorder*. Unpublished doctoral dissertation, University of Leeds, Leeds, UK.

Wright, H. C. (1997). Developmental coordination disorder: A review. *European Journal of Physical Education, 2*, 5-22.

Wright, H. C., & Sugden, D. A. (1996a). A two step procedure for the identification of children with developmental coordination disorder in Singapore. *Developmental Medicine and Child Neurology, 38*(12), 1099-1106.

Wright, H. C., & Sugden, D. A. (1996b). The nature of developmental coordination disorder: Inter and intra group differences. *Adapted Physical Activity Quarterly, 13*, 358-374.

Wright, H. C., & Sugden, D. A. (1996c). The nature of developmental coordination disorder in children aged 6-9 years. *Journal of Sports Sciences, 14*, 50-51.

Wright, H. C., & Sugden, D. A. (1997). Management of children aged 6-9 years with developmental coordination disorder. In I. Morisbak & P. E. Jorgensen (Eds.), *Proceedings of the 10th international symposium on adapted physical activity, 1995* (pp. 287-311). Oslo/Beitostolen: ISAPA.

Wright, H. C., & Sugden, D. A. (in press). A school based intervention programme for children with developmental coordination disorder. *European Journal of Physical Education, 3*.

Wright, H. C., Sugden, D. A., Ng, R., & Tan, J. (1994). Identification of children with movement problems in Singapore: Usefulness of the Movement ABC Checklist. *Adapted Physical Activity Quarterly, 11,* 150-157.

Wright, H.C., & Thorpe, R. (1989). The effect of different knowledge of result regimen on the learning of a motor skill in a school situation. *Physical Education Review 12,* 164-167.

INDEX

ABOUT THE AUTHORS

David A. Sugden is Professor of Special Needs in Education at the School of Education, University of Leeds. He originally trained as a teacher in England before spending 5 years at UCLA obtaining higher degrees and working in the area of special education. He specifically focused on children with physical difficulties, studying and working with Professor Jack Keogh. His research work has concentrated on developmental issues and applying these to children with physical difficulties. He moved to Leeds University in 1977, becoming Senior Lecturer in 1985, Reader in 1990, and Professor of Special Needs in Education in 1992. His research interests span the full range of special education, examining issues such as inclusion, provision for named disabilities, and teaching approaches. However, his specific interest is physical disability, with ongoing projects involving preschool assessment measures for DCDs and hand function in children with hemiplegic cerebral palsy. He is author of numerous books and articles on motor development and motor impairment.

Helen C. Wright, PhD, is Senior Lecturer at the School of Physical Education, Nanyang Technological University, Singapore. She originally trained as a physical education teacher at St. Mary's College, Strawberry Hill, UK, and began her career as a physical education teacher in the UK and Jordan. After 8 years of teaching school children, from grade 1 through grade 13, she returned to study for an MSc at Loughborough University, UK, before moving to a lecturing position at Nanyang Technological University, Singapore. She has worked there for the past 10 years, becoming a senior lecturer in 1998 and teaching courses on motor control, motor learning, and motor development. Her interest in children with movement difficulties began when she returned to the UK for 3 years to study for her PhD at the University of Leeds with David Sugden. On her return to Singapore, she has continued to write on the nature of the difficulties that children with DCD experience.